BARNES & NOBLE BASICS™

knitting and crocheting

by Nancy J. Thomas

**BARNES
& NOBLE
BOOKS**

NEW YORK

For information, contact:
Barnes & Noble, Inc.
122 Fifth Avenue
New York, NY 10011
212-633-4000

Other titles in the **Barnes & Noble Basics**™ series:
Barnes & Noble Basics *Using Your PC*
Barnes & Noble Basics *Wine*
Barnes & Noble Basics *In the Kitchen*
Barnes & Noble Basics *Getting in Shape*
Barnes & Noble Basics *Saving Money*
Barnes & Noble Basics *Getting a Job*
Barnes & Noble Basics *Using the Internet*
Barnes & Noble Basics *Retiring*
Barnes & Noble Basics *Using Your Digital Camera*
Barnes & Noble Basics *Getting Married*
Barnes & Noble Basics *Grilling*
Barnes & Noble Basics *Giving a Presentation*
Barnes & Noble Basics *Buying a House*
Barnes & Noble Basics *Volunteering*
Barnes & Noble Basics *Getting a Grant*
Barnes & Noble Basics *Getting into College*
Barnes & Noble Basics *Golf*
Barnes & Noble Basics *Your Job Interview*
Barnes & Noble Basics *Résumés and Cover Letters*
Barnes & Noble Basics *Starting a Business*
Barnes & Noble Basics *Personal Budgeting*
Barnes & Noble Basics *Home Renovation*
Barnes & Noble Basics *Diabetes Cookbook*

introduction

"All of a sudden I'm seeing people knitting and crocheting every-where," said my cousin April. "My friends say it's a great way to relax and spend time together, too—they even go to 'knitting salons'! I'd love to learn, but I'm afraid I'm just not coordinated enough."

Wrong! Anyone can learn to knit and crochet—it doesn't take any special talent, just a desire to learn. Of course, a good instruction manual helps too, and that's where **Barnes & Noble Basics** *Knitting and Crocheting* can help. In just a few short chapters, you will have all the basic stitches mastered, and soon you will be on your way to turning out your own stylish accessories, sweaters, and more!

Knitting and Crocheting starts with the basics, such as picking the right yarn and needles and making sense of needlecraft patterns. Then it leads you step-by-step through the build-ing blocks of knitting and crocheting. Each step is fully illustrated, and each chapter is chock full of resources for learning more.

Next, you can try your hand at twenty super quick and easy knitted and crocheted projects. You even get full-color photos of all the finished projects to inspire you. Check out the gorgeous afghan on page 170 and the great striped scarf on page 180. Yes, these are beginner projects that anyone—even you—can learn to make!

Learning to knit or crochet has never been easier. So turn the page and see why needlecrafts are back in vogue again!

Barb Chintz
Editorial Director, the **Barnes & Noble Basics**™ series

table of contents

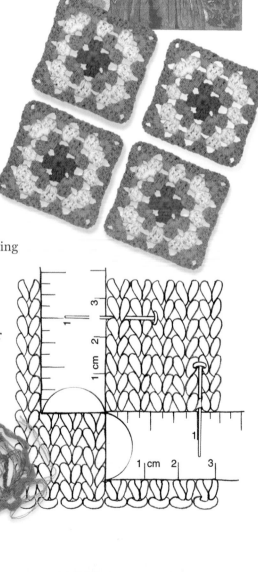

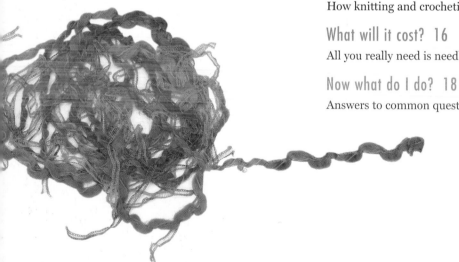

Chapter 1
THE CRAFT

knitting vs. crocheting

It's just needles or hooks —and stitches

So you've decided to learn to knit or crochet! Well, you're certainly not alone: These crafts have never been more popular. And with just a little practice and patience, even a beginner like you can learn to turn out stylish, one-of-a-kind pieces in a flash.

Of course, like any hobby that requires learning a new skill, knitting and crocheting can seem daunting at first, especially if you have friends who can already stitch up intricate creations overnight. But don't worry! Once you learn a few basic stitches, you will be matching them stitch for stitch in no time.

Before you start learning the basics, it's a good idea to understand the difference between knitting and crocheting. In simple terms, knitting requires two needles (in most cases), while crocheting uses only one hook.

The two crafts are alike in that the fabric that results is made from a single continuous strand of yarn. By making and joining rows of stitches, you can create everything from scarves and blankets to stuffed toys and slippers.

Crocheted items are made of loops joined into a row, and these rows are joined to one another one stitch at a time. In general, crocheting creates a firmer, less flexible material than knitting, although the result depends on the type of yarn used and the size of the hook.

Knitted items are also made of interlocking loops joined row to row. But instead of working with only one stitch at a time, you keep all of the stitches on the needle while you work. Then you simply transfer them from one needle to the other as you go along. Knitted fabric can certainly be firm, but knitting is usually a better choice if you want to create a more flexible fabric for soft items such as sweaters and afghans.

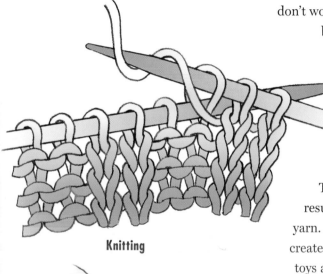

Knitting

Crocheting

ASK THE EXPERTS

I've tried quilting and embroidery, but gave up because they were too hard. What can I expect with knitting and crocheting?

Everyone can learn to knit or crochet—even children! It's really not that difficult. With a ball of yarn, some inexpensive tools, and basic instructions, you'll be off and running. Practice and the desire to learn are all you really need to master these needlecrafts. And unlike quilting and embroidery, it won't be months before you finish your first project; you can create a simple scarf in several hours. Good luck!

How long will it really take me to become skilled at knitting or crocheting?

After working your way through the first few chapters of this book, you should be well on your way toward grasping the basic stitches and techniques. The more advanced techniques are all built on the basics, so once you get the hang of those, your skills will quickly improve. As with anything else, there's a learning curve to needlecrafts, but the more you practice, the easier it becomes.

When can I start my first project?

Believe it or not, once you learn the basic stitches, you'll be ready to tackle your first knitted or crocheted project. But start simple. While you may really want to make a fancy sweater, it's easier to begin with a scarf or a hat. Once you've completed an easy project, it will give you more confidence to go on to the next level.

origins of knitting and crocheting

When you learn to knit or crochet, you'll become part of a rich tradition that stretches back centuries. Plus, you'll join the growing ranks of knitting and crochet aficionados around the world.

Have you ever wondered about the history behind these two needle-crafts? Many of the knitting styles we use today, including the style used for fisherman's sweaters, Aran knits, and the Fair Isle technique, originated in the British Isles and Scandinavia. Legend has it that sailors wore sweaters with their family pattern knit into them so that their bodies could be identified if they died at sea.

Other knitting techniques, including a little-known looping technique known as nälbinding, originated centuries earlier in the Middle East. Few pieces of early knitting still exist because the technique was used mostly to make basic garments that were worn until they fell apart; also, knitted garments disintegrate quickly in humid climates.

The face of knitting changed dramatically when the knitting machine was invented during the Industrial Revolution. Knitting ceased to be a cottage industry mostly done by men and gradually developed into the leisure activity, mainly practiced by women, that we know today.

The history of crochet is just as long and varied as that of knitting. The word *crochet* comes from the French word for a "small hook," and in the early years it was mostly done with fine thread and tiny hooks. The result was the intricate lace that was used as finery and trim on garments—especially on religious robes.

A form of crochet called "nun's lace" was known as far back as the Middle Ages in Europe, but it really flourished in the mid-1800s in the British Isles. These days, lace making has almost disappeared, and crochet has evolved into a hobby that uses yarn and larger hooks to create garments, accessories, and soft furnishings such as throws and pillows.

Crochet was probably introduced to Ireland by way of France in the late 1700s, but it was not widely practiced until around 1830, when crocheted items became popular—partly because all that was required was a simple hook and inexpensive but durable cotton thread. The wives of fishermen and laborers began crocheting small items to supplement the family income. During the infamous Potato Famine of 1845–50, these crocheted items played an integral role in helping many families survive. They used savings made from selling their crocheted work to purchase boat passage to America or Canada to escape the famine and start new lives. Ironically, though, once in the New World, many Irish lost interest in crochet and the practice dropped off.

why needlecrafts?

A great way to beat stress

Chances are you're no stranger to stress. Whether you are a busy executive running between meetings or a soccer mom chauffeuring your children around town, you could probably use a few new ways to relax.

This is where knitting and crocheting can help; both are said to work wonders when it comes to soothing nerves and relieving anxiety. In *Zen and the Art of Knitting,* author Bernadette Murphy claims that needlecrafts evoke the classic "relaxation response," which includes lowered heart rate and blood pressure.

In this era of New Age health practices, needlecrafts are also emerging as an ideal way to explore your spirituality and creativity. Some even go as far as calling knitting the "new yoga," and many swear by its meditative benefits. Needlecrafts are good for the ego, too: Finishing a tough project will give you a great feeling of accomplishment.

WHY SHOULD YOU LEARN TO KNIT OR CROCHET?

- It's a great way to beat stress
- It has a calming and meditative effect
- Finishing a project will give you a great sense of accomplishment
- It's an easy way to socialize and make friends
- You can create beautiful, meaningful gifts for friends and family
- You can take it anywhere
- It's inexpensive, easy to learn, and requires few tools
- It can help add balance to a hectic, high-tech lifestyle
- It will make waiting or killing time pleasant and constructive
- It's a great way to express your creativity
- You can create items for charity or sell them at bazaars

Knitting and crocheting are also the perfect antidote to one of life's necessary evils: waiting. Because needlecrafts are so portable, many people bring their projects along when they know they'll have some time to kill. What better way to pass those long minutes waiting for an appointment than by adding a few rows to a scarf? Instead of feeling the usual restlessness, you'll enjoy a relaxed frame of mind while actually getting something constructive done.

And consider this: Needlecrafts can actually help you kick a bad habit, such as overeating or smoking. You can't eat or smoke while your hands are busy with needlecrafts, and the meditative rhythm will calm any anxiety you might feel at the loss of your old crutch.

Finally, don't overlook the powerful pleasure that comes from making something beautiful and original with your hands. As our world grows increasingly high-tech and more of us spend all day working on computers, expressing your creativity in a hands-on way can be especially gratifying.

FIRST PERSON SUCCESS STORY

A Stitch in Time

In the past few years I've suffered two devastating losses in my family. For a while, it seemed like nothing could lift my grief. But then two months ago a concerned friend signed me up for a knitting class, and it's really been a lifesaver. I find the simple repetitive movements of knitting very comforting and soothing, like fingering "worry beads." Whenever I feel sad, I just pick up my knitting and concentrate on keeping my stitches even. And when I travel for work, I take my knitting with me on the plane or train. Imagine my surprise last week when I realized that all this knitting has paid off: I've managed to complete a beautiful multicolored sweater, on top of learning a great new way to beat the blues.

—**Tina H., Newcastle, PA**

which one to learn?

Knitting or crocheting— or both?

At this point, you're probably wondering which to learn first, knitting or crochet. And you're probably trying to make that decision based on which one is easier. Well, in truth, they're about the same in terms of difficulty. Whether you use two needles (knitting) or one hook (crochet), it's possible to master the basic stitches of both in no time flat. Honest!

You may want to experiment with both needlecrafts first to see which one you enjoy more. In the end, the deciding factor may be what you're most interested in making. If you love the idea of making one-of-a-kind throws for yourself or to give as gifts, or you want to make baby blankets for your pregnant friends, crocheting may be the needlecraft for you. On the other hand, if you want to make mittens, scarves, and sweaters, knitting is probably the way to go.

However, you may find that knowing both knitting and crochet comes in handy. Many needlecrafters learn both and use them at different times, even combining them in the same project. Or you may find that you naturally gravitate toward the one your friends or family do. You might pick up crocheting because your favorite aunt does it, or you might learn to knit because all your friends are in a knitting circle. Just remember: Whichever you choose, you definitely will not be alone!

ASK THE EXPERTS

Is it possible to learn to knit and crochet at the same time?

Sure, it's possible, but it's probably a better idea to start with one needlecraft and practice it until you are proficient before picking up the other one. In the long run, you will be a better knitter or crocheter if you take your time and get the basics down first, rather than trying to do too much at once.

I'm left-handed. Will it be harder for me to learn to knit or crochet?

No, not necessarily. Both left-handers and right-handers will experience a bit of awkwardness at the beginning, as both these needlecrafts are two-handed skills. So, the best thing to do is simply to learn as any right-hander would, since you'll end up using both hands anyway. In the long run, learning this way will make it easier for you to follow written instructions and illustrations, which are based on a right-handed approach. Then, with a little practice, you'll soon be flying along and keeping pace with the right-handers—and even surpassing them!

I like the idea of crocheting, but I don't want to end up with some stiff, unyielding fabric. Is it also possible to crochet softer, more flexible fabric, perfect for afghans and sweaters?

Yes. While crocheting is often used to make firm projects like bags, it is a very versatile craft. By using thicker yarn and a larger hook, it is possible to create a more loosely looped textile, and crochet that soft and scrunchy shawl that you're looking for.

What are some examples of combining knitting and crocheting in the same project?

Knitters often use crocheted edges to complete garments and home décor items. It is very easy to crochet simple, stable finishes along the edges of knit items, and knitters appreciate having these easy techniques at their fingertips to complete their knitting projects. Occasionally, crocheters will use knit edgings on projects, but this is less common.

what will it cost?

Get started for little outlay

If you're like most people, you have a limited amount of money to spend on leisure activities, so taking up an expensive hobby is probably the last thing you want to do. But if you're thinking of taking up knitting or crocheting, you're in luck—the basic requirements for these needlecrafts are few. You can get started with just an inexpensive skein of yarn and a pair of needles or a hook. Of course, as you become more skilled, you will want to add some other helpful tools and try out some more interesting and expensive yarns.

Even when you are new to the crafts, though, you should get the best yarn you can afford. Making a project with a more attractive, quality yarn will give your confidence an added boost. Plus, you will have a project that you will be proud to wear or to give as a gift.

This does not mean that your first attempt has to be expensive, however; there are many yarns out there that are both affordable and high quality.

You can buy yarns, tools, books, and other supplies in a variety of ways. You can purchase them at mass retailers like Michael's or Jo-Ann's or through specialty yarn shops. The prices at the mass retailers are lower, but they have a more limited selection of natural fiber yarns. Specialty shops offer better customer assistance to help you select your yarn and supplies, but the final cost may be higher. You can also make purchases at online stores or through catalogs like Herrschners, Mary Maxim, Patternworks, and Lion Brand Yarns. All catalogs have connected Web sites.

Consumer events and shows also offer some excellent buying opportunities. The best-known events are the Stitches show (**www.knittinguniverse.com/xrx/Events.asp**) and the Knitting Guild of America conventions (**www.tkga.com**).

Knitting and crocheting are two of the most affordable hobbies out there. The total cost for making something depends largely on the type of fiber used and the finished size of your project. For example, a scarf made with a textured acrylic yarn will cost you about $6, $20 if you use a hand-dyed wool, and $60 or more if you use variegated plush rayon fiber. These costs may also vary depending on whether you buy your yarn at a mass retailer or specialty shop. Here's a look at some typical project costs.

Project	Mass retailer or low-end yarn	Moderate specialty shop or yarn	High-end specialty shop or yarn
Scarf	$6–12	$15–25	$40–60

Scarves can often be made with just a ball or two, depending on the yardage of the yarn and the length and width of the finished scarf.

Hat	$5–8	$10–20	$30–45

Depending on the type and yardage of the yarn, you might even have enough to make both a hat and a scarf for these prices.

Pullover	$15–20	$25–60	$70–170

Based on a long-sleeved, medium-sized women's pullover sweater.

Kid's sweater	$8–15	$20–30	$35+

Based on a sweater for a child 2 to 6 years old.

Throw	$20–45	$50–80	$90–140

Beautiful multiyarn decorator throws fall into the higher price category.

Baby blanket	$13–20	$30–40	$50+

These generally fall in the low-to-moderate price range because they are made of sturdy yarns that are machine washable and dryable.

now what do I do?

Answers to common questions

I always thought knitting was for little old ladies, but my 20-year-old daughter just joined a knitting circle! Why is it suddenly so popular again?

In the last several years, the world of needlecrafts has been revitalized by the introduction of fun novelty yarns and trendier patterns, and the revelation that even movie stars (Julia Roberts and Kate Hudson, for example) have taken it up. Knitted and crocheted accessories are also making a comeback on the fashion scene. Finally, bigger needles and larger hooks, along with thicker yarns, provide the instant gratification that today's needlecrafters desire.

I tried to learn to crochet once when I was younger, but quickly gave up. How can I make learning easier on myself?

There are many options for beginners, so you might want to experiment to find the method that works best for you. You can study one-on-one with a teacher, take a class, watch a video, learn from a book, or take tutorials on the Web. In fact, a combination of these methods might be the answer for you. You might also want to buy a kit that provides all the materials you need to learn the craft and to make your first project. Some of these kits even include videos.

As a beginner, I don't find knitting very relaxing! I get very tense and afraid I'll drop a stitch. Is this normal?

This is completely normal for a beginner. The relaxing and meditative qualities of knitting and crocheting won't "kick in" until you feel more comfortable with your work. Practice helps a lot, so just keep at it. It really does get much easier as you go along.

NOW WHERE DO I GO?

WEB SITES

KNITTING HISTORY

www.shetland-knitwear.com
Click on "History"

www.aranknitting.com

www.geocities.com/invtex
Click on "History" under "Knitting Technology"

www.redcross.org/museum
Click on "American Red Cross Knits"

CROCHET HISTORY

www.victoriancrochet.com
Click on "Crochet History"

www.librarycompany.org/hookbook
Click on "Historical Reflections in Crochet"

www.crochet.org/newslet/
nl0997a.html

BOOKS

KNITTING HISTORY

Poems of Color:
Knitting in the Bohus Tradition
By Wendy Keele
Explores the history of a workshop in Sweden that
created world-famous Bohus designs for more than
half a century. Includes patterns for beautiful
sweaters using this technique.

A History of Handknitting
By Richard Rutt
The former Bishop of Leicester in the U.K.,
Richard Rutt (a.k.a. "The Knitting Bishop") has
written what is arguably the best book about the
vast history of knitting.

Knitting Ganseys
By Beth Brown-Reinsel
Learn about the rich sweater-knitting tradition of
British fishermen and create your own gansey.

CROCHET HISTORY

Crochet History & Technique
By Lis Paludan
The definitive tome that everyone quotes, this book
is chock full of great black and white photos and
illustrations of techniques.

Donna Kooler's Encyclopedia of Crochet
By Donna Kooler
A relatively new entry, this general resource book
covers yarn, tools, and basic techniques, and
includes an informative chapter on crochet's history.

A Living Mystery: The International Art
and History of Crochet
By Annie Louise Potter
An in-depth history book written by the respected
founder of Annie's Attic, a mail-order crochet business and publisher of crochet booklets.

Chapter 2

YARNS AND TOOLS

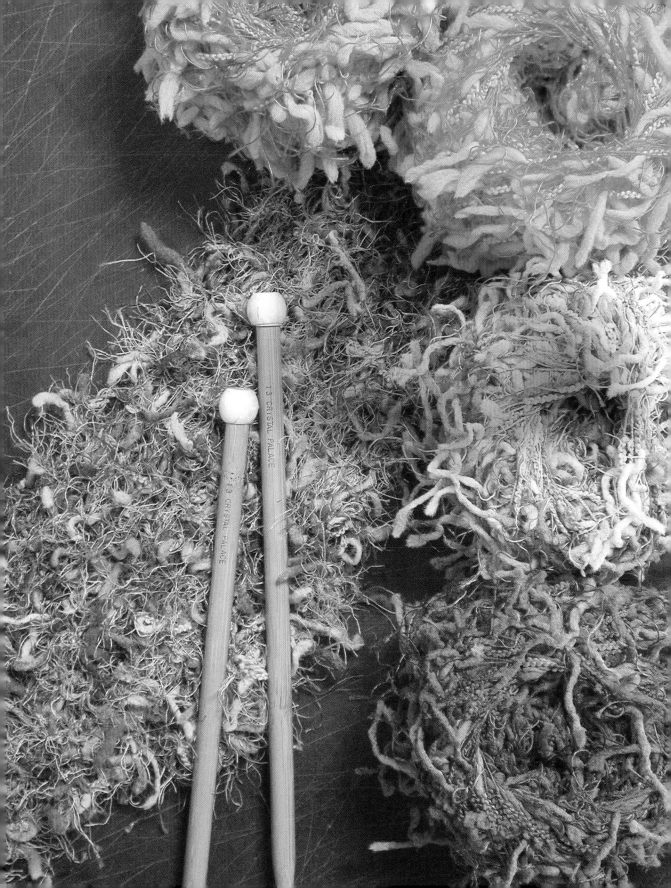

yarn 101

Ball   **Skein**   **Hank**

All wound up

Learning about yarn is an essential part of learning to knit or crochet. Along with knitting needles and crochet hooks, yarn is an indispensable ingredient. Yarn is made up of various fibers that are spun into a variety of thicknesses.

Yarn is commonly packaged in a ball, skein, or hank. Some cotton yarn and ribbon yarn comes wrapped around a cardboard cone. When making something, try to purchase all the yarn you will need at one time. Yarn is dyed in lots (the number of the dye lot is noted on the label). Because there are slight color variations from lot to lot, always choose balls of yarn from the same dye lot.

You will find lots of helpful information on the yarn label, including the weight of the yarn, given in ounces and grams, and the yardage, given in yards and meters. As you become more experienced, you'll understand how helpful this information is when you want to find out how much yarn you need for a specific project (see page 50).

The label also gives you the fiber content of the yarn and how to care for it. Some yarns are machine washable, while others require hand washing.

On the label you may also find information about the size of the knitting needles or crochet hooks that work best with the yarn. This is just a suggestion, but it will give you a good place to start.

A   Photograph of final project
B   Weight in ounces and grams
C   Length in yards and meters
D   Suggested knitting needle and crochet hook sizes
E   Fiber content
F   Care instructions
G   Dye lot number

UNDERSTANDING YARN WEIGHTS

Yarn comes in various weights (thicknesses), from very thin threadlike string to extra-thick strands. What you are making will determine the weight you choose. And the size of the needles or hook you use depends on the thickness of the yarn.

There are six general yarn weight ranges. You will probably be working with the last three, heavier ranges for most of your beginning projects. The weights here don't assume any particular texture or fiber type.

A Super Fine This weight is used to make lace shawls, fine baby wear, and socks. It can also be labeled sock-, fingering-, or baby-weight yarn.

B Fine While not as thin as the super fine, it is again primarily used for very lightweight pieces such as socks and baby garments. It can also be called sport weight or baby yarn.

C Light Lightweight yarn is used for lighter sweaters. You will sometimes find this weight called DK (double knitting in British terminology) or light worsted weight.

D Medium This is a versatile yarn that can be used for sweaters and home décor items. It is often called worsted weight.

E Bulky Using this weight allows you to finish projects more quickly. You will need to use a larger needle or hook size with this thickness. It is also known as chunky or craft yarn.

F Super Bulky This is the thickest weight and is usually for outerwear and accessories. It might be called super chunky or roving yarn. Obviously this makes for the fastest projects.

Yarns are shown at actual size

yarn fibers

The first time you search for yarn, you may be overwhelmed by the selection. It's less intimidating when you break the choices down into three basic fiber types—animal, plant, and synthetic.

Wool, the most popular animal fiber, comes from sheep. Wool is a good choice because it is warm, durable, and has thermal qualities that wick moisture away from your body. It is also reasonably priced. You may notice there are differences in the softness of wool yarns. The grade of wool and the brand of sheep's fiber make all the difference. If you want softer wool, look for labels that say Merino or lamb's wool.

Wool yarn is easy to work with. Any unevenness that occurs as you knit or crochet disappears after you wash the garment.

Other animal fibers include mohair and cashmere from goats, angora from angora rabbits, and alpaca from the South American alpaca, a llama-like animal. Mohair is the warmest and fuzziest of these fibers, and angora is also soft and hairy. Alpaca and

cashmere are relatively flat in appearance, although both are incredibly soft. These are luxury fibers, so you may find them blended with other fibers, including wool, which reduces the cost.

Cotton is the best-known plant fiber. It does not have the elasticity of wool, so complete a few projects before you tackle cotton yarn. Linen yarn, although not as popular, can be found. Other plant fibers, such as hemp, are not commercially available in yarn form for use in needlecrafts.

Synthetic fibers are also easy to work with. During World War II, yarn shortages drove scientists to develop synthetics that mimic natural fibers. Today, advances in the fibers have made them mainstays for many knitters and crocheters. They are inexpensive and most are machine washable and dryable. Common varieties include acrylic, polyester, and nylon.

The fibers from alpaca (left) and sheep (below) make warm and durable garments.

fun yarns

Beyond the basics

Once you get plugged into the world of needlecrafts, you will see that one of the great reasons to knit or crochet is that you get to work with some really fun yarns. Using novelty yarns, you can make unique items that you would never be able to find in a store. Basic yarns are very important and will never be replaced by novelty yarns, but novelty blends add excitement to knitting and crocheting. Yarns with nubs of color, furry strands, and unusual mixtures of fibers are some of the varieties you are likely to encounter.

Variegated yarn has dyed areas of different colors within the same ball. There are both inexpensive machine-dyed ("space-dyed") varieties and costlier hand-dyed types. When worked, these yarns make a striped or patterned fabric, depending on the length of color repeated along the strand of yarn. You'll love working with variegated yarns because you can make incredible-looking projects with minimal skill.

Printed yarns have one main color with splotches of others throughout. Some baby yarns made with this process result in a finished product with a dotted appearance.

Heather yarn is a solid yarn made by twisting several complementary shades of yarn together. Marled yarn is made by twisting several contrasting colors.

Eyelash yarns are fuzzy, with many short, wispy strands. This creates dimension and gives a furry look to the finished item. They are used alone or in combination with other yarns, and also come in variegated varieties.

Bouclé or loopy-textured yarns create a dimensional fabric. While these yarns cover imperfections in your knitting or crocheting, they can be a challenge to work with if you are a real beginner.

Roving and handspun yarns have a loose twist and are often made of wool or wool blends. They are easy to use, but may pull apart slightly as you work. And because they are loosely spun, some amount of pilling (the formation of tiny fuzzy balls) can occur.

knitting needle basics

More than just two sticks

KNITTING NEEDLE CHART

Knitting needles come in both American number sizes and metric sizes. Most needle packages give both numbers.

US	Metric
0	2 mm
1	2.25 mm
2	2.75 mm
3	3.25 mm
4	3.5 mm
5	3.75 mm
6	4 mm
7	4.5 mm
8	5 mm
9	5.5 mm
10	6 mm
10 ½	6.5 mm
11	8 mm
13	9 mm
15	10 mm
17	12.75 mm
19	15 mm
35	19 mm
50	25 mm

When you start knitting, a simple pair of straight needles is ideal. As you get more in tune with the knitting world, you will begin to see that there are many needle options. None are better or worse; it's really a matter of preference. Over time, you will develop your own favorites when it comes to needles.

Basically, knitting needles come in three varieties: straight, circular, and double-pointed. Within these categories you'll find a dizzying array of lengths, thicknesses, and materials.

Knitting needles can be made of plastic, metal, wood, or bamboo. Some metal needles are coated with plastic. As a beginner, look for needles that are less slippery. Plastic and wood are two good choices. They keep stitches from falling easily off the needles as you knit.

Straight needles come in pairs in two basic lengths—10" and 14". The shorter are good for projects that don't have too many stitches. The longer can be used for most project types. Buy the 14" variety if you want the most versatile needles without having to purchase an extensive number of them.

A circular needle consists of two needles joined at one end by a connecting cord. They are used for projects with large numbers of stitches, such as throws. They can also be used for circular items such as hats and sweater bodies. Short varieties are used to make neckbands. Their main "claim to fame" is that using them eliminates the need for a sewn seam.

Double-pointed needles have points on both ends and come in sets of four or five. They are used for smaller tubular accessories, such as mittens and socks. Don't consider using these until you feel comfortable with straight needles.

KNITTING NEEDLE TIPS

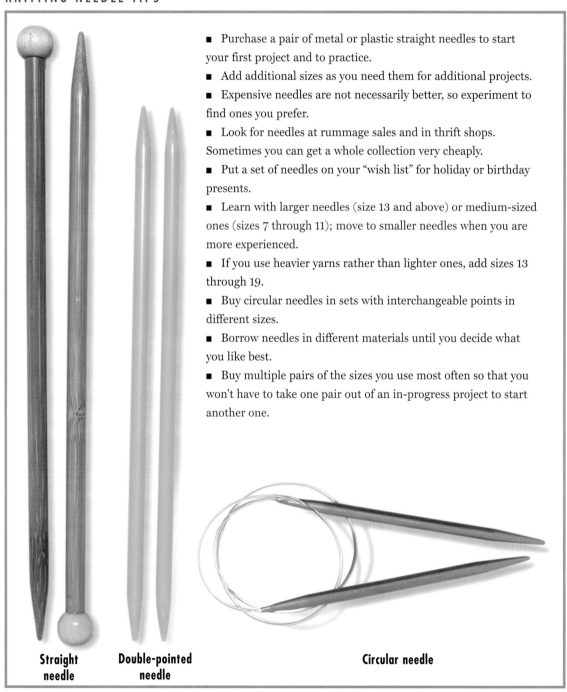

- Purchase a pair of metal or plastic straight needles to start your first project and to practice.
- Add additional sizes as you need them for additional projects.
- Expensive needles are not necessarily better, so experiment to find ones you prefer.
- Look for needles at rummage sales and in thrift shops. Sometimes you can get a whole collection very cheaply.
- Put a set of needles on your "wish list" for holiday or birthday presents.
- Learn with larger needles (size 13 and above) or medium-sized ones (sizes 7 through 11); move to smaller needles when you are more experienced.
- If you use heavier yarns rather than lighter ones, add sizes 13 through 19.
- Buy circular needles in sets with interchangeable points in different sizes.
- Borrow needles in different materials until you decide what you like best.
- Buy multiple pairs of the sizes you use most often so that you won't have to take one pair out of an in-progress project to start another one.

Straight needle

Double-pointed needle

Circular needle

crochet hook basics

Start with the right tools

A crochet hook is a straight, tubular, sticklike tool with a small curve or hook on one end. As with knitting needles, there are a variety of sizes available, and they come in plastic, metal, and wood. Most crochet hooks are about 6" long, with the exception of the very largest sizes, which are slightly longer.

You may encounter some hooks that have special ergonomic features to make them easier to hold and use. These are ideal if you spend lots of time working on computers and want to avoid repetitive stress injuries to your hands.

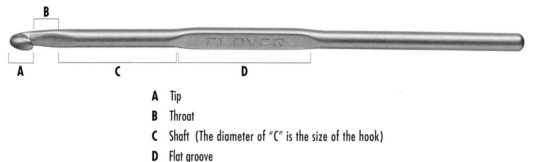

A   Tip
B   Throat
C   Shaft (The diameter of "C" is the size of the hook)
D   Flat groove

A crochet hook has four distinct parts. Starting at the top is the tip or hooked part. This portion is rounded on some hooks and flatter on others. This is the part that allows you to pull a loop of yarn through a stitch. Below the hook is a short area called the throat, which makes it easy to wrap the yarn as you make stitches. Next is the shaft. If you don't know the size of your hook (some do not have the size printed on them), you can measure the metric diameter of this area, then use the chart on the next page to figure out the letter size. Further down is a flat groove where you place your fingers to hold the hook. The remainder of the hook is a tubular handle that adds balance and a place to rest your hand.

Crochet hooks are sold singly or in sets. You are most likely to use hooks in the middle range, from size G-6 and up. Small hooks are used with finer yarns and are generally not used by beginners.

CROCHET HOOK CHART

Crochet hooks come in both American number sizing and metric sizing. Most hook packages give both numbers.

US	Metric	US	Metric
B-1	2.25 mm	I-9	5.5 mm
C-2	2.75 mm	J-10	6 mm
D-3	3.25 mm	K-10.5	6.5 mm
E-4	3.5 mm	L-11	8 mm
F-5	3.75 mm	N-13	9 mm
G-6	4 mm	P-15	10 mm
H-8	5 mm	Q-19	16 mm
		S-35	19 mm

ASK THE EXPERTS

My grandmother has passed on to me a set of very thin steel hooks. How are they used?

Steel hooks are almost antiques these days. They were used with fine cotton thread to make beautiful, labor-intensive doilies and bedspreads. Today, only the most avid crocheters work with them.

My crochet hooks have only metric (mm) sizing on them and my pattern calls for hooks with letter sizes. What should I do?

Use the crochet hook chart above to match the mm number on your hook with the appropriate letter sizing. Manufacturers sometimes include only one measure or the other, though some include both.

Is it more difficult to use the jumbo (size P or Q) hooks?

Not only is it not difficult, but it is sometimes easier than using a regular size hook, depending on the yarn you choose. And because of their size, these hooks will let you crochet much, much faster.

necessary accessories

**Helpers that make
needlecrafting easier**

As you start knitting or crocheting, you'll soon find that you need a few little accessories. While some of these are not essential, they do make the process more enjoyable.

Needle/hook measure and stitch gauge tool   One of the first accessories you should pick up is a little all-purpose tool that measures the diameter of needles and hooks, as well as your stitch and row gauge (see pages 66–67 for more on gauge). It also has a short but handy ruler for measuring in inches and centimeters.

Stitch markers   Markers are used to segregate stitches and mark various areas in your knitting projects. They come in two varieties. Solid rings, often used in knitting, fit onto a needle and set off stitches, making it easier to keep track of stitch patterns. Open-and-close markers can be put into finished fabric; for this reason, these work especially well in crocheting, in which no "live" stitches are left on the needle as they are in knitting.

Sewing needles   Usually, you use the same yarn that you used for your project to close the seams of an item made from yarn. For easy sewing, as well as for weaving in yarn ends, you will need a special large-eyed, blunt-point needle. These come in either plastic or metal. Long crafting pins called T-pins are used to hold the seam in place as you sew.

Cable needles   These short needles, which help you knit cables, have points on both ends and come in plastic, metal, or wood. Some have a curved section in the center to hold stitches in place as you make the cable (see pages 124–125 for more on cables).

Row counters   As you graduate to more advanced projects, you will want to keep track of the number of rows you have worked for specific projects. Row counters track up to 99 rows and come in the handheld variety and the type that fits onto your knitting needle.

Stitch holders   These look somewhat like giant safety pins and are used to hold a row of unfinished stitches for completion later, often with a different color yarn (see the sweater on page 120).

Must have

- Scissors or snips
- Retractable tape measure (**A**)
- Large-eyed, blunt needles for seaming (**B**)
- T-pins for seaming

Should have

- Needle/hook and gauge measure tool (**C**)
- Stitch markers (**D**)
- Stitch holders (**E**)
- Cable needles (**F**)

Nice to have

- Row counter (**G**)
- Safety pins (to use in place of markers or for marking button placement)
- Needle or point protectors (to keep stitches from falling off the needles between sessions)

Frills, but nice to have

- Blocking board and blocking pins (to shape finished projects)
- Ball winder to make hanks into balls
- Curved seaming needles (for easier seaming)
- Cutting pendant for plane travel (cuts yarn but does not have an exposed sharp edge)

Using what you have

- Contrasting yarn ring for markers
- Safety pins for stitch holders
- Rubber bands for needle protectors
- Double pointed needle in place of a cable needle
- Sticky notes for keeping your place in a pattern

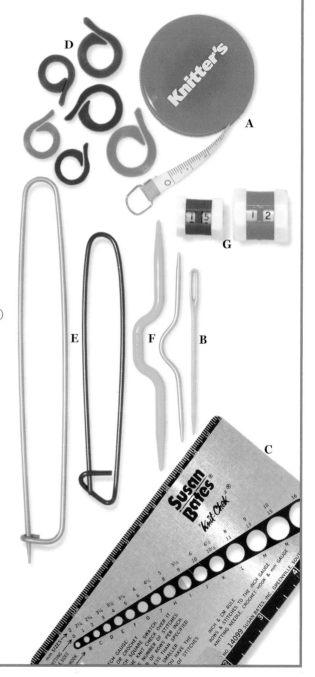

storage options

Putting it all together

Almost before you begin your first lesson, finding ways to organize your yarn, needles/hooks, and other paraphernalia will become a necessity. You can use what you have on hand or buy specially made storage items. For example, you can keep your crochet hooks in a resealable plastic bag or purchase an organizer designed to hold a large number of hooks.

Store yarn in a dry, clean place out of direct sunlight. Once you purchase more than a few balls, you will want to find a way to keep track of it. Clear plastic tubs are ideal. You can store by color, fiber, or some combination of both. Once you become a real "yarn collector," it is helpful to keep a notebook with a strand of yarn and information such as the number of balls you have, dye lot, place and date purchased, etc.

Some knitters and crocheters like to keep their tools right at hand, so storing them in open jars or vases works well for them. If you want to travel with your tools, consider buying a flat holder, which is available for both needles and hooks.

The other temporary storage device that is almost indispensable for needlecrafters is a tote designed for carrying both yarn and tools. Some come with zippered pockets to keep tools and accessories organized. Ultimately, when you have several projects in progress at the same time, you may want to have more than one of these.

THE NEEDLECRAFTER'S NOTEBOOK

Keeping records of your projects is satisfying and helps when you want to make a repeat of an item. A loose-leaf notebook is perfect for this. Keep a sample of the yarn and attach the band from the yarn ball. If you are super-organized, take a photo of the finished item and attach it to your needlecraft diary.

Totes

For under $10 you can buy a basic tote. A midrange tote costs about $25 and luxury styles go for $50 and up. Look for quality straps and details such as pockets with zippers. Some totes are built with a grommet in one end so that you can thread the yarn through it and keep it organized as you work.

Standing totes

If you want to set up your needlework next to your favorite armchair, get one of these. They keep your projects off the floor and give you a more permanent storage place. Some models are made so that you can take the tote off the stand for travel.

Straight needle cases

The material used to make the needle case is reflected in the cost of the case. You can find them in everything from plastic to fine tapestry material. These cases come in zippered and nonzip varieties.

Circular needle holders

Circular needles are a challenge to organize. One type of holder allows you to organize your needles by size and hang them from a clothes hanger. Other holders are made like CD cases, with plastic pockets to keep the needles from tangling.

Crochet-hook and double-pointed needle cases

These are shorter versions or the regular straight needle cases. For about $20 to $25 you can get a very good case. If you have all three types of needles, matching cases are a nice touch.

Rolling crafting stand

You can purchase one designed for needlecrafts or buy one from your local office supply store. Look for one with several drawers for organizing books, accessories, yarn, and other supplies.

now what do I do?

Answers to common questions

I'm just starting to knit and want to get some yarn for my first project. What kind is best?

Buy a smooth, light-colored yarn that makes it easy to see the stitches. Don't start with a very fine yarn or eyelash yarn. A thick yarn and big needles will get you going much faster and will be easier for you to use as you learn.

I want to start by making a baby blanket for a gift, but I don't want to use traditional pastels or plain yarn. What are my options?

There are many options available for making a baby blanket, just keep in mind that you want a yarn that is easy to launder. You can use a washable wool, a textured acrylic, or even a cotton yarn. Try a variegated yarn that will create a fun pattern as you knit. If the blanket is a gift, put in a yarn label so that the parents will know how to wash it.

I've noticed that some knitting needle tips are blunt and others are pointed. Which kind is better?

Try out both types and decide for yourself. Some knitters like a pointed tip, others like the more rounded variety.

My grandmother gave me her old needles. Are they still good to use?

Knitting with your grandmother's needles would certainly be a nostalgic experience, so look the needles over. Sometimes plastic needles warp and metal ones get damaged by wear or because they haven't been stored carefully. The stitches should always slide easily and any needle with a rough or damaged tip should be discarded.

I just purchased a yarn that is 50 percent wool and 50 percent acrylic. Is this better than using a yarn that is 100 percent wool or acrylic?

It's really a matter of taste. However, blending yarn does tend to bring out the best properties of each fiber. Blending wool with acrylic results in a less expensive, easy-care yarn that is also warm and absorbent.

Why is cashmere yarn so much more expensive than wool?

It is really a matter of supply and demand. There are a lot more sheep that produce wool than there are goats from which to gather cashmere fibers. Plus, these goats live in remote mountainous areas, so even gathering the fiber is difficult. Sheep also have much fuller coats, so a greater quantity of wool can be taken from one coat.

I washed my sweater in hot water and it shrunk! How can I keep this from happening again?

To avoid shrinking your sweaters, eliminate agitation and heat. Hot water and the agitation of your washing machine can cause the fibers to meld together and shrink. However, some people actually want their knitted items to shrink and meld to create items such as slippers and bags; this process is called felting (see pages 110–111). Felting only occurs with yarns made from animal fibers.

I'd like to knit with wool, but I've heard that it is difficult to launder. Is this true?

Not necessarily. If you want easy-care yarn, look for the term "superwash" on the yarn label. Yarn treated with this process can be washed by machine and often machine dried. Also, many new wool washes, such as Eucalan and Woolite, make it easy to care for items made of untreated wool. It's as easy as throwing them into your washing machine on a gentle cycle and then drying them flat. Some washes don't even require rinsing.

NOW WHERE DO I GO?

WEB SITES

www.yarnshoppe.com

www.woolconnection.com

www.patternworks.com

www.lionbrand.com

http://halcyonyarn.com

www.artfibers.com

www.knitlist.com
Click on "Tools"
A thorough list of handy accessories for knitting and crocheting.

BOOKS

Knitting for Dummies
By Pam Allen
Good overall information
plus info on tools and yarns.

A Passion for Knitting
By Nancy J. Thomas
and Ilana Rabinowitz
Contains a comprehensive section on yarns and everything you need to get started, as well as all the basics.

Chapter 3

GETTING STARTED

ways to learn

Different strokes for different folks

Everyone learns in different ways and, not surprisingly, at different speeds. And, as the truism goes, what works for you may not work for the next person.

This is definitely the case when it comes to needlecrafts: No one method is 100 percent effective for every learner. Before you jump in, think about how you prefer to learn. Do you learn best from illustrations? From verbal instructions? Once you know your learning style, the next step is to find an instructional method that complements it.

There are four basic approaches to learning needlecrafts:
1. **Visual:** illustrations in books and on Web sites
2. **Interactive visual:** CD-ROMs or videos
3. **Verbal:** written or spoken instructions
4. **Hands-on:** classes

For many, a combination of a few of these ultimately works best.

The plus of visual learning methods is that you can go at your own pace and examine the path of the yarn strand and the stitch placement in the illustrations. You can also pause or rewind a video or CD-ROM if you need to look at a step more closely. The drawback of visual methods is that there is some room for interpretation, and because no one is watching you, you may end up learning a technique incorrectly without realizing it.

If you're primarily a verbal person and are able to "get" concepts from words, then written instructions may work well for you. However, a combination of words and illustrations is probably a better approach for most.

If you're the kind of person who grasps new ideas better in an interactive setting, then classes might be the way to go. You'll get a hands-on approach to learning, plus the teacher can demonstrate the stitches and give you feedback. The only drawback to learning this way is that your teacher won't be with you when it's time to practice. A back-up book is a good solution to this learning dilemma.

Many of the booklets, books, and CD-ROMs listed below are available from the yarn manufacturers' Web sites listed on page 37.

Booklets

These are inexpensive (often under $10) and cover very basic techniques. All include easy projects.

The All New Teach Yourself to Knit
Learn to Knit in Just One Day
Learn to Crochet in Just One Day
10, 20, 30 Minutes to Learn to Knit
10, 20, 30 Minutes to Learn to Crochet

Books

Books are more expensive, but cover a wider range of techniques and projects.

The Knitting Experience, Books One and Two, by Sally Melville et al.
How to Knit by Debbie Bliss
Knitting for Dummies by Pam Allen
The Complete Idiot's Guide to Knitting and Crocheting, (Second Edition) by Barbara Breiter and Gail Piven

CD-ROMs

CD-ROMs are good for the visually minded, but are not usually project oriented.

Knitting Made Easy
Crocheting Made Easy
The Easy Way to Learn Knitting
The Easy Way to Learn Crocheting

Web sites

These sites all include illustrations and instructions on basics.

www.learntoknit.com
www.vogueknitting.com/tech/knit/knit.html
www.knitting.about.com
www.learntocrochet.com
www.crochet.about.com
www.crochet.org/lessons/lesson.html

first steps

Getting past the awkward phase

Don't worry if the knitting needles or crochet hook still feel foreign in your hands. Any new skill takes time to learn, and all learners go through an awkward stage. You may be struggling a bit right now, but rest assured that when it clicks (and it will), you will forget about those clumsy first stitches.

And don't be concerned about how you're holding the needles right now either, or worry that you're not doing it in exactly the right way. As times goes on and you get more practice, you will perfect your holding position. The most important thing at this point is that you feel comfortable.

And look at it this way: Once you finish that first lesson, it just gets easier from there. Your first lesson will probably be challenging, because you'll be learning how to hold your tools and make basic stitches. In car lingo, you are going from zero to 60 miles per hour in one lesson. But it never gets harder than that. From that day on, you'll just be building on that first lesson.

As you go along, you'll learn new stitches based on the first ones, and soon you'll be able to start your first project. You'll also learn how to correct errors such as a dropped stitch.

Do try to work your stitches correctly in the beginning. If you start off working in an incorrect way, it gets more difficult to correct the longer you continue. If you can get a knowledgeable knitter or crocheter to look at your technique as you work, he or she can help you get on the right track.

As you begin to feel more comfortable with the process, look for better ways to hold the yarn so that you can add speed to your skills. It may come naturally to you, but if it doesn't, check out the helpful diagrams in some beginning knitting and crochet booklets.

10 QUICK TIPS FOR SUCCESS

1. Relax and make it fun.
2. Don't compare yourself to others.
3. Expect to need a refresher after your first lesson.
4. Choose smooth, light-colored yarns for your first project.
5. Ask for help when you need it.
6. Keep going, even if your piece is not perfect.
7. Keep your expectations reasonable and your goals obtainable.
8. Look for learning aids to help you.
9. Pick an easy first project.
10. Proudly say, "Yes, I made it," when asked about your needlework!

the needlecraft community

Finding buddies and mentors

Meeting friends and teachers who share your passion for knitting and crocheting is easier than you think, and it's a great way to check your progress and learn new techniques.

The Web is a good place to start. Search for knitting or crocheting groups. Some groups have planned agendas and meetings, while others are more laid back, with people simply getting together to chat and share their craft.

There are also national and local knitting and crocheting guilds. The national groups host conventions and seminars where you can take classes and meet people from around the country. The Knitting Guild of America (TKGA) and the Crochet Guild of America (CGOA) are the two major U.S. guilds, and both put out periodical publications. Joining a local guild lets you connect with others in your area and take workshops, while also giving you entree into the larger national guild world.

HOPE FOR LEFT-HANDERS

Even if you're left-handed, it is best to learn to knit or crochet exactly as right-handers do. It helps that knitting is really an "ambidextrous" craft that uses right and left hands almost equally. Any awkwardness will soon disappear as you practice and gain confidence, and learning this way will give you a big advantage as you go beyond the basic techniques, because just about everything you will find is illustrated, written, and designed for right-handed needlecrafters.

There are also consumer-oriented needlecraft events and fairs throughout the year in various cities. The most famous one is a conference/trade fair called Stitches. Stitches has three major events—East, West, and Midwest—where you can take classes, see what other needlecrafters are doing, and purchase goodies. They also run several "camp," or retreat, programs. Some smaller groups so look forward to the yearly fairs that they charter buses to get there. More on Stitches can be found at **www.knittinguniverse.com**.

If you don't have time to get involved in a needlecraft group, but still want answers to your questions, consider subscribing to an online group such as the Knitlist (**www.knitlist.com**) or Knit U (found at **www.knittinguniverse.com**). Crocheters can go to **www.groups.yahoo.com/group/crochetlist**.

Another way to meet folks is by asking at your local yarn or craft shop. Or try asking work buddies if they want to take classes with you, and pretty soon you'll have your own group of knitting or crocheting "newbies."

FIRST PERSON SUCCESS STORY

There Is No "Right" Way

I've been teaching for a number of years and have successfully taught many students. One of my left-handed students had a real block about learning to knit. I told her to stop thinking of her left-handedness as a stigma, and that there was no reason she couldn't learn in the same way a right-handed knitter learns. Knitting is a two-handed process, I reminded her, and any initial clumsiness soon goes away. Not only did my student become a knitter, but she became an extraordinary knitter who now teaches others.

—Daniele T., Colorado Springs, CO

needlecraft lingo

Learning the language of knitting and crocheting

As you start learning to knit and crochet, you'll soon be immersed in a world of new words and abbreviations. When you begin, many of the terms appear to be in an unfamiliar new language. For example—how do you say "skein"? Those in the know say "skane," not "skeen."

Some of this language is used in written patterns and instructions. Other terminology—for example, when talking with another knitter about a stockinette stitch pullover—is simply a matter of the way you discuss knitting and crocheting.

Go slowly, just as you would when learning a foreign language. Start with the basics and then progress to more complex terminology. Generally, beginner patterns spell out terms and use fewer abbreviations than those for more experienced knitters and crocheters. A glossary (see page 194) and abbreviations list (see page 197) can be extremely helpful for beginners.

Weights and measures that relate to yarn packaging are also abbreviated. The most common ones that you'll encounter are oz (ounce), g or gr (gram), yd (yard) and m (meter). The other two metric measures are mm (millimeter) and cm (centimeter).

NEEDLE CHAT

If you get involved in Internet chat rooms you'll find some funny terms used—KIP for knitting in public, UFO for unfinished objects, or WIP for work in progress. It doesn't take long to figure out what's what. In such chat groups, knitters and crocheters talk a great deal about yarn collecting (stash enrichment) and what they want to make, are making, or plan to make. These terms are not used in an instructional way, but are knitting and crocheting slang.

ASK THE EXPERTS

Why do knitting patterns use abbreviations? It would be so much easier if everything were written out.

Knitting and crocheting instructions, especially those found in knitting and crocheting magazines, use abbreviations to save space. Some abbreviations are intuitive, such as "st" for stitch, while others—like "sc" for single crochet or "RS" for right side—may be a bit more confusing. The good news is that most abbreviations are standardized.

How can I keep track of abbreviations and terms when I'm working on a project?

Make a copy of your pattern so that you can mark it up and make notes in the margins. You can also highlight terms and specific areas so you will be able to follow along more easily. Some people also find it helpful to write out the full words for their first projects.

My crocheting pattern is so confusing! It has lots of *, [ ], and (). What are these symbols?

These symbols are used to segment areas that are repeated a certain number of times. For example, "*single crochet twice next single crochet; repeat from the * 5 times more" means that you work this stitch sequence a total of 6 times. Learn more about these symbols on page 198.

I bought some patterns on my European vacation. Will these instructions use the same terms and abbreviations as those used in the United States?

Many terms are similar, but with slight variations. For example, British knitting patterns say "cast off " and American patterns say "bind off." Do take care when using crochet patterns from Britain, as they have a different crochet stitch sequence (an American single crochet is called a double crochet in Great Britain and Ireland, and an American double crochet is a British treble.)

your first project

Up to this point, you have just been preparing to begin to knit or crochet. Starting with the next chapter, you'll actually get down to the business of knitting. So now is the time to make your final preparations—choosing your yarn and your project.

Yes, you can actually make a simple project as you learn. Basic hats and scarves make good first projects. To make it even easier, pick a project that is done in one stitch and one color, such as the scarves on pages 68 and 150. Avoid projects that have a lot of finishing, other than a simple seam to sew or an end or two of yarn to weave in.

Choose yarn that is thick enough to allow you to clearly see your stitches and the corresponding needles or hook. Simply put, you want to have yarn and tools that will allow you to create nice, even stitches. It shouldn't be a struggle.

Pick a lighter-colored shade of yarn, avoiding colors such as black and navy. You can also use a variegated yarn shade. Actually this is a plus, because the variation in color is fun to work with. Also make sure to choose a flat, untextured yarn. Textured yarns will be more enjoyable once you've become more skilled.

Stick with wool, acrylic, or a blend of the two fibers for your first project. Don't buy an expensive luxury yarn until you have a little bit of experience. When in doubt, enlist the help of a teacher, yarn store employee, or another knitter to help you choose a yarn that is suitable for a beginner.

ASK THE EXPERTS

I found a yarn I like that is pretty plain, but it does have flecks of color in it. Is this okay to use for my first project?

Give it a try. Tweed yarns with flecks of color aren't complicated to use—even for a beginner. You can also try yarns with a two-color twist, sometimes called "ragg" or marled yarns. Just avoid lots of texture that hides your stitches as you knit or crochet.

Can I buy a kit that will have everything I need to begin?

Absolutely! There are a number of kits available for both knitting and crocheting, created with beginners in mind. Most include tools and instructions, as well as yarn. Some kits even include videos. You can find these kits in catalogs, in shops, and online. If you have limited access to shops, this is a very good way to get started. These make great gifts for friends, too, and there are even kits for children. Most kits are designed so that you can do a project or projects with the included yarn. The only drawback with kits is that you don't get to choose your yarn type or color.

pattern speak

You may decide to start learning with a store-bought pattern instead of one in this book. Patterns are found in lots of places, including magazines, booklets, books, and the Internet. Some are even free.

If you're looking for a pattern to start with, you might be wondering what you need to know, and how to read patterns in general.

Most patterns include the same information, even if it comes in a slightly different format. Most patterns will include information such as:

A. Skill level   Look for beginner or easy patterns. If no skill level is given, read through the pattern to see if it includes stitches that you understand and doesn't involve complex shaping.

B. Size   Items such as accessories usually come in one size. Sweaters are given by sizes—sometimes simply small, medium, or large—or in chest measurements (such as 36", 38", 40"). Children's garments often are sized by age.

C. Finished Measurements   This is the real determinant of what size to make. If you consider yourself a small, but want a loose-fitting sweater, you may really want to make a medium or even a large.

D. Materials   This part provides guidelines on yarn, tools, and notions such as buttons. Note that where it gives needle or hook sizes, it may also say "or size to get gauge." This means that you may need to use a different-sized hook or needles to make your project come out the correct size. Learn more about gauge on page 66.

E. Gauge   This measurement is the number of stitches and rows you need to aim for when making a 4"-square sample (gauge swatch) before starting your project. Getting the gauge right will help you end up with a finished item that's the right size. See page 66 for more on gauge.

F. Notes   Additional information about the pattern. Read this section carefully before you begin working.

G. Pattern pieces   The directions are usually broken down according to the various pieces you'll need to make. With sweaters, directions for the back are usually given before the other pieces, followed by the front and then the sleeves.

H. Finishing   This section tells you how to put your pieces together and add neckbands, edgings, and embellishments.

NOTES ABOUT THIS PATTERN

The pattern on the opposite page features sweatshirt-style sweaters for both children and adults. The photo of the pattern shows the finished sweaters. The bolded areas of the pattern are the headings and important details, such how to work specific rows. Abbreviations such as St st, inc, and rib are explained in the glossary that starts on page 194. You'll be learning these techniques in chapters 4, 5, and 8.

LION BRAND® HOMESPUN® HOODED KNIT SWEATERS

EASY

SIZE
Child's 2 (4, 6-8, 10-12); **Adult's S (M, L, 1X, 2X, 3X)**
Finished chest 26 (29, 32, 35)"; **38 (41, 45, 49, 53, 57)"**

NOTE
Adult sizes in bold appear following child's sizes. For ease in working, circle all numbers pertaining to your size.

MATERIALS
• LION BRAND Homespun
  2 (2, 2, 3); **3 (4, 4, 5, 5, 6)** skeins of color of your choice shown in:
  MAN – #363 Sandstone
  WOMAN – #315 Tudor
  GIRL – #351 Caribbean
  BOY – #355 Delft
  BABY – #356 Everglade
• Sizes 8 (5 mm) and 10 (6 mm) knitting needles OR SIZE TO OBTAIN GAUGE
• Large-eyed, blunt needle

GAUGE
12 sts + 18 rows = 4" (10 cm) in St st (k on RS, p on WS) with larger size needles. BE SURE TO CHECK YOUR GAUGE.

NOTE
If desired, work Hood and edging with a circular needle.

STITCH EXPLANATION
3-needle bind off With RS together, hold in one hand two needles with equal number of stitches on each. With third needle, knit tog one st from each needle; *knit tog one st from each needle, pass first st worked over second to bind off; rep from * across to last st. Cut working yarn and pull through last st to secure.

BACK
With smaller needles, cast on 40 (44, 48, 52); **58 (62, 68, 74, 80, 86)** sts. Work in St st for 4 (4, 4, 4); **6 (6, 6, 6, 6, 6)** rows. Work in k1, p1 rib for 4 (4, 4, 4); **6 (6, 6, 6, 6, 6)** rows. Change to larger needles. Work in St st until piece measures 15½ (16½, 17½, 18½)"; **24 (25½, 27, 27½, 29, 30½)"** from beg or desired length. Place all sts on spare needle or holder.

FRONT
Work same as Back until piece measures 13½ (14½, 15½, 16½)"; **22 (23½, 25, 25½, 27, 28½)"** from beg, ending with a WS row.
Shape neck: Next row (RS) K 17 (18, 19, 20); **22 (23, 25, 27, 29, 31)** sts, join a 2nd ball of yarn and loosely bind off center 6 (8, 10, 12); **14 (16, 18, 20, 22, 24)** sts, k 17 (18, 19, 20); **22 (23, 25, 27, 29, 31)** sts. Working both sides at the same time with separate balls of yarn, bind off 2 sts at each neck edge once, then dec 1 st at each neck edge every other row twice. Work even until same length as Back to shoulder. Work 3-needle bind off on 13 (14, 15, 16); **18 (19, 21, 23, 25, 27)** sts for each shoulder seam. Bind off center Back 14 (16, 18, 20); **22 (24, 26, 28, 30, 32)** sts.

SLEEVES
With smaller needles, cast on 20 (22, 24, 24); **28 (28, 30, 30, 30, 30)** sts. Work in St st for 4 (4, 4, 4); **6 (6, 6, 6, 6, 6)** rows, then in k1, p1 rib for 4 (4, 4, 4); **6 (6, 6, 6, 6, 6)** rows. Change to larger needles. Work in St st, inc 1 st each edge of second RS row, then every 4th row 9 (10, 10, 11); **12 (13, 13, 14, 15, 16)** more times – 42 (44, 46, 48); **54 (56, 58, 60, 62, 66)** sts. Work even until Sleeve measures 11 (12, 13, 14)"; **16 (17, 17, 18, 18, 18)"** from beg or desired length. Bind off loosely.

HOOD
With RS facing and larger needles, pick up and k 32 (34, 38, 42); **46 (50, 54, 58, 62, 66)** sts around neck, starting at right side of neck and leaving center 6 (8, 10, 12); **14 (16, 18, 20, 22, 24)** sts free. Work in St st, inc 10 (10, 8, 6); **6 (6, 6, 6, 6, 4)** sts evenly spaced across first row, until Hood measures 8½ (9, 9½, 10)"; **12 (12, 12, 13, 13, 14)"** – 42 (44, 46, 48); **52 (56, 60, 64, 68, 70)** sts around neck. Placing half of Hood sts on 2nd needle, work 3-needle bind off across Hood top seam.
Facing edging With RS facing and smaller needle, pick up approximately 55 (57, 59, 61); **67 (67, 67, 73, 73, 77)** sts around front edge of Hood. Work in k1, p1 rib for 4 (4, 4, 4); **6 (6, 6, 8, 8, 8)** rows. Work in St st for 4 (4, 4, 4); **6 (6, 6, 8, 8, 8)** rows. Bind off loosely on last row with larger needle. Sew rib/roll Front at center neck, overlapping center fronts (left over right for male; right over left for female).

FINISHING
Mark 6½ (7, 7½, 8)"; **9 (9½, 10, 10½, 11, 11½)"** down from each shoulder seam. Sew Sleeves to body between markers. Sew side and Sle_____ ms. At roll edge of Sleeves and body, reverse_____ ___ ___t_r roll. Weave in ends.

Front and Back (Child)

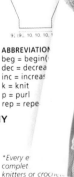

Sleeve (Adult)

ABBREVIATION___
beg = begin(___
dec = decrea___
inc = increas___
k = knit
p = purl
rep = repe___

LION BRAND® YARN
"Famous for Quality Since 1878"
LION BRAND®YARN COMPANY
New York, New York 10011 U.S.A.
Visit us at our Website for free patterns and copy of our yarn guide:
www.LionBrand.com

LB #10520
Homespun (Article #790) comes in 6 oz/185 yd skeins

*Every e___
complet___
knitters or croche___

51

now what do I do?

Answers to common questions

When I sign up for a class, will supplies be included?

Some beginner classes include yarn and needles for practice. Generally, though, you'll need to purchase yarn and needles for your first project. Whether your class provides materials or not, you'll still get advice on buying supplies. Always ask about what you need before your first class.

I bought a book to learn to knit, but I can't seem to follow the illustrations. What should I do?

Keep the book for reference and find a CD-ROM or video or take a class where someone can show you exactly how to do what you see in your book.

I can't find the yarn called for in my scarf pattern. Can I use another yarn?

Yes, but choose a yarn that has the same texture and weight if you want similar results. Use approximately the same size needles, or the needles listed on the yarn label. Your gauge swatch will determine if the substitute works. If you get the same gauge, you are good to go ahead. If you don't get the same gauge, experiment with needle/hook sizes until you do.

I just started my first project and I know I'm going to have a lot of leftover yarn. Plus, I just bought some great new yarns to try out later. What's the best way to keep track of the yarn I'm starting to amass?

For most serious knitters, having a yarn collection is the inevitable result of loving and buying yarn. There are many ways to store your yarn collection—you just need to find one that will let you put your hands on the yarn when you need it. Some knitters store their yarn by color, fiber, or type of yarn. It is important to keep your yarn in a clean and dry place. Plastic tubs or cardboard boxes make good storage containers. Consider clear plastic if you want to be able to see what you have at a glance. Once your yarn supply gets larger, it is helpful to keep a notebook with details of what you have, the number of balls, and where it is stored, along with sample strands.

NOW WHERE DO I GO?

WEB SITES

www.knitting.about.com

www.crochet.about.com

www.tkga.com

www.crochet.org

www.knitlist.com

www.knittinguniverse.com

MAGAZINES

Family Circle Easy Knitting

Better Homes and Gardens Knit It!

Vogue Knitting

Knitter's

Knit 'N Style

Interweave Knits

Cast On

Crochet

Crochet Fantasy

Chapter 4
KNITTING BASICS

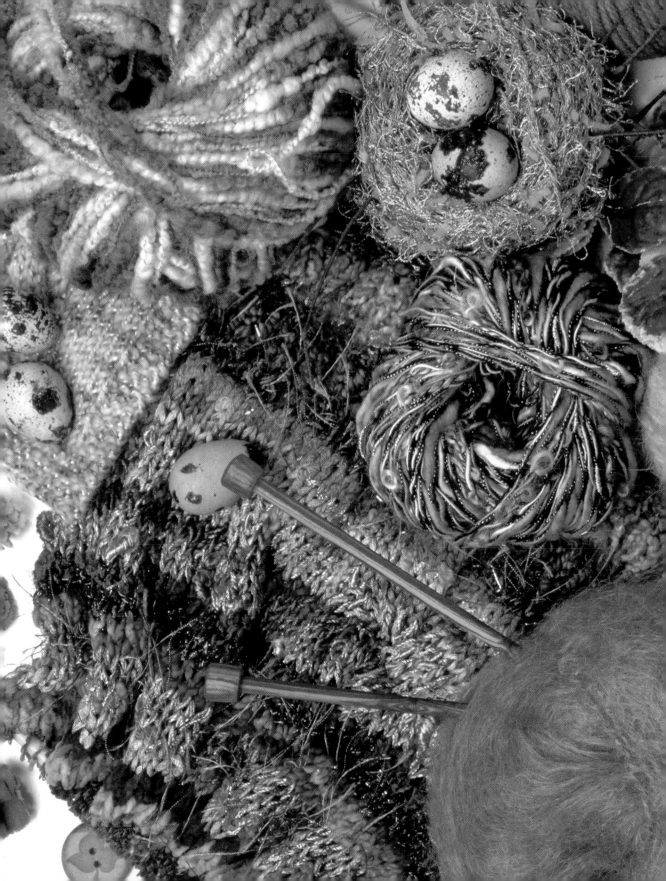

casting on

Putting stitches on the needle

You're just about ready to put those first stitches on your needles and start knitting. Don't panic—it's much easier than it seems, and soon you'll look back on these first steps and laugh at how you thought you'd never get it.

The very first stitch you'll need to master—and it's a cinch—is the slipknot. This is what anchors the yarn on your needle. Why a slipknot and not a regular knot? A slipknot is ideal because it can easily be adjusted to fit any size needle.

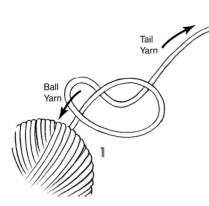

Tail Yarn

Ball Yarn

1

Here's the easiest to way to make a slipknot:

1. Pull about six inches of yarn from your ball or skein. This is the yarn "tail." Create a loop in the middle of the strand, and place it on top of the tail.

2. Holding the loop and the tail together in one hand, use one knitting needle to pull the tail strand up through the loop. As you pull it up, tighten the slipknot onto the needle.

2

Great, you did it. Now you'll need to learn how to cast on. This is the foundation of any knitted piece and the key to getting off to a good start.

There are many ways to cast on, but the easiest one to start with is probably the "knitted cast on," which is described on the next page. As you work through the steps, make sure you don't cast on too tightly, or inserting the needle into the first row of knitting will be difficult.

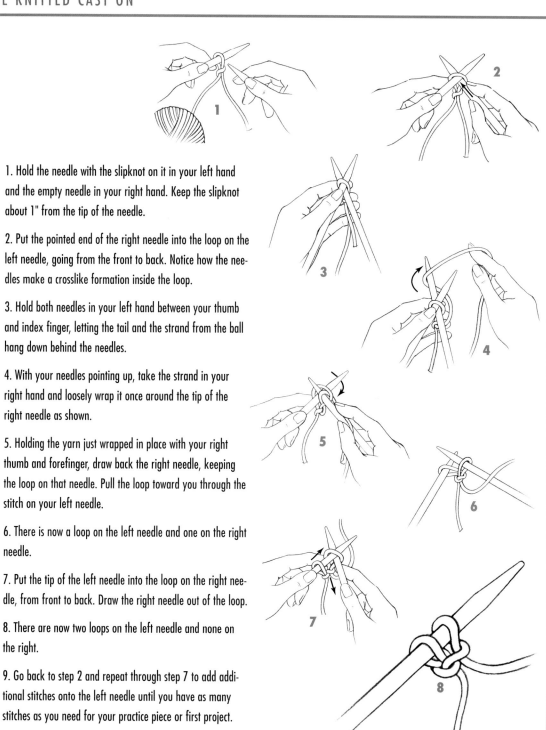

1. Hold the needle with the slipknot on it in your left hand and the empty needle in your right hand. Keep the slipknot about 1" from the tip of the needle.

2. Put the pointed end of the right needle into the loop on the left needle, going from the front to back. Notice how the needles make a crosslike formation inside the loop.

3. Hold both needles in your left hand between your thumb and index finger, letting the tail and the strand from the ball hang down behind the needles.

4. With your needles pointing up, take the strand in your right hand and loosely wrap it once around the tip of the right needle as shown.

5. Holding the yarn just wrapped in place with your right thumb and forefinger, draw back the right needle, keeping the loop on that needle. Pull the loop toward you through the stitch on your left needle.

6. There is now a loop on the left needle and one on the right needle.

7. Put the tip of the left needle into the loop on the right needle, from front to back. Draw the right needle out of the loop.

8. There are now two loops on the left needle and none on the right.

9. Go back to step 2 and repeat through step 7 to add additional stitches onto the left needle until you have as many stitches as you need for your practice piece or first project.

the knit stitch

The grandmother of all stitches

In knitting, there are really only two stitches—the knit stitch and the purl stitch. Everything in knitting is based on these two stitches, and with just the knit stitch, in fact, you can make a variety of projects.

The knit stitch is the foundation for all other stitches, so once you have this one down, all the other stitches will be that much easier to learn.

In the knit stitch, you basically move all the stitches from the left needle onto the right in order to work a row (that's "knit speak" for completing one row of stitches).

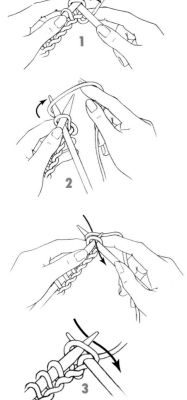

The knit stitch follows all the same steps for casting on, except for the last step:

1. Hold the needle with the stitches cast on it in your left hand, and hold the empty needle in your right hand. Insert the empty needle into the center of the stitch closest to the tip of the left needle, just as you did when you cast on.

2. Hold both needles in your left hand and with your right hand wrap the yarn around the tip of the right needle as shown.

3. Secure the wrapped yarn with your right hand and tighten the stitch slightly, then pull the right needle back through the stitch, pulling up a loop onto the right needle.

Now here's where the knit stitch differs from casting on:

4. Now, simply slide the loop on the left needle off the end of the needle. This will leave the stitch on the right needle. One stitch has been knit.

Repeat steps 1–4 until all the stitches have been knit and one row is done.

Now you are ready to start a new row. Transfer the empty needle to your right hand and the needle with the stitches to your left hand. Your working yarn will be at the beginning of the new row, near the tip of the needle.

When you knit every stitch in every row, you're using what's called garter stitch. Garter stitch fabric is spongy, flexible, and will not roll. It makes a good stitch for a scarf or hat. It is very easy to count rows in garter stitch, as each ridge is composed of two knit rows.

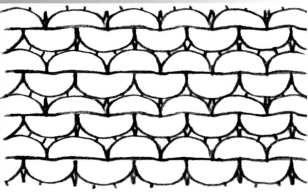

Four Fast Steps

When it comes down to it, knitting requires just four basic steps. Try repeating to yourself "Insert-Wrap-Pull-Slide" as you go along, and soon you'll be knitting with the big kids!

1. INSERT Insert the right needle into the stitch on the left needle.

2. WRAP Wrap the yarn around the right needle.

3. PULL Pull through a loop of yarn.

4. SLIDE Slide the loop on the left needle off, leaving a completed stitch on the right needle.

the purl stitch

The second basic stitch

You're ready to move on to your second stitch—the purl stitch. Purl stitches are a great accompaniment to knit stitches. Most knitted pieces are a combination of knit and purl stitches. You'll soon see for yourself how perfectly they work together.

Purling requires the same four easy steps used in knitting, but the way you handle the yarn and form the stitch is slightly different. When you knit, you keep the strand of yarn from the ball behind your needles. When you purl, the yarn is placed in front of the knitting.

NOTE: Don't get tense! As you practice your first stitches, try to keep an even tension. This means that you should not pull the yarn too tightly as you form the stitch, nor leave it too loose. Uneven tension is a common problem for beginners, but one that you can help prevent by paying attention to how tightly you are pulling.

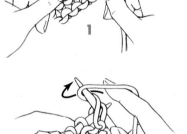

The purl stitch can be broken down into five basic steps:

1. As with the knit stitch, you start out with the stitches in your left hand and the empty needle in your right hand. However, keep the yarn in front, as shown. Then, insert the right needle into the first stitch, from right to left.

2. Wrap the yarn around the right needle as shown. Notice how this is different from step 3 of the knit stitch (see page 58).

3. Hold the yarn in place with your right forefinger and thumb and gently pull the right needle backward out of the stitch on the left needle, drawing through a loop.

4. Slide the loop off the left needle, which leaves a new stitch on the right needle. You have completed one purl stitch.

Repeat steps 1–4 until you finish the row.

THE STOCKINETTE STITCH

Once you can knit a row and purl a row, you are ready to put the two together to create the most basic stitch in knitting: the stockinette stitch. You do this by knitting the first row and purling the next one. After a few rows, you will start to see the difference between the front (right) and back (wrong) sides of your piece. The right side consists of flat, V-like knit stitches, while the wrong side is made of bumpy purl stitches. Being able to distinguish the right from the wrong side will help you figure out where you are when you pick up your knitting to begin a new row. If the V-side is facing you when you place the needle with stitches on it in your left hand, you should knit the row, and you should purl a row if the bumpy side is facing you.

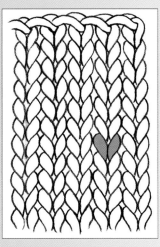

Right (knit) side

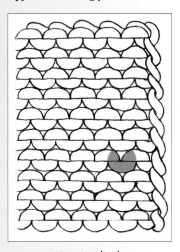

Wrong (purl) side

Counting Rows

Counting the rows you knit doesn't need to give you a headache. There are several simple ways to do it. You can count rows on the piece of knitting itself, mark the number down on a piece of paper as you go along, or use a row counter. If you count them on the fabric, remember that it's much easier to do on the knitted V-side of your piece.

quick tips and hints

Staying on top of the learning process

As you learn your first stitches, bear in mind that you will get stuck at some point. However, everyone encounters a small setback or two during this phase, so take comfort in the fact that your problem has probably been faced by beginners everywhere at some point.

These quick answers to common beginner problems will help make your first attempts go more smoothly.

How do I start a new row without adding extra stitches?

Adding extra stitches is a very common beginner's mistake. To prevent this, be sure to take the yarn under the needle and not over when you start a new row. Here are the correct and incorrect ways to start a new row using knit and purl stitches:

| WRONG | CORRECT | WRONG | CORRECT |

| Knit side taking the yarn over the needle. | Knit side the correct way. | Purl side taking the yarn over the needle. | Purl side the correct way. |

Why are my edge stitches so big and loopy?

For now, don't worry if your first and last stitches are bigger than the rest. This is a common problem for beginners and it will go away as you become more experienced.

How do I find my place if I put my knitting down in the middle of a row?

Next time, try to finish the row before you set down your knitting. But if you're stuck now, pick up the piece and turn it so that the yarn is coming from the right needle. Are the stitches Vs or bumps? If they are Vs, knit the rest of the row. If they are bumps, purl the remainder of the row.

How do I measure a knitted piece?

When measuring a knitted piece that's still on your needles, be sure to lay it flat. Measure across to get the width and vertically (not diagonally) to get the length. Don't include the stitches on the needle, as those will become the next row.

IF YOU DROP A STITCH

As a new knitter (and even an experienced one), you are bound to drop a stitch every now and then, but don't let it panic you. If it falls off without unraveling, simply put the tip of your needle into the stitch and slip it back onto the needle. Take care not to twist the stitch. Another tip: It helps to count the stitches in your rows now and then to make sure you haven't lost any stitches.

To fix a dropped stitch that has unraveled:
Even if your stitch drops off and unravels, you can still reunite the stitch with the stitches on your needle using a crochet hook. The size of the crochet hook is not that important.

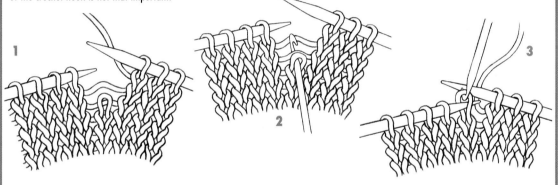

1. Knit to the place where you have dropped the stitch.

2. Use a crochet hook to fix the stitch by putting the hook through the stitch and drawing the first strand of yarn through the loop. Continue to insert the hook and draw through the strands of yarn until all the rows are worked and your stitch is back where it belongs.

3. Slip the stitch onto the needle and finish knitting the row.

To fix a dropped stitch that has not unraveled:
1. Knit stitch: Using the right needle, lift the stitch and move it onto the left needle. Then knit the stitch.

2. Purl stitch: Using the right needle, lift the stitch and move it to the left needle. Then purl the stitch.

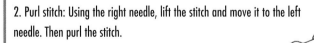

binding off

The big finish

Congratulations! You've mastered the basic stitches and are just about to finish your first piece. But you're sitting there with the piece in your hands and the yarn still on the needle, wondering how to finish it off. No problem.

When you are at the end of a piece, you need to finish it by binding off the stitches. You'll want to do this loosely, so that the edge does not become too tight and pull in.

These are the basic steps for a clean finish:

1. Knit the first two stitches in the last row.

2. Insert the left needle into the front of the first stitch on the right needle and pull it over the second stitch. One stitch is left. Knit the next stitch and the insert the needle into the first stitch again and pull it over the second stitch.

3. Repeat this across the row until one stitch remains on the right needle. Snip the yarn, leaving a short tail (of about 4 or 5") that you will weave into your fabric. Draw the end of the tail through the last stitch to secure it.

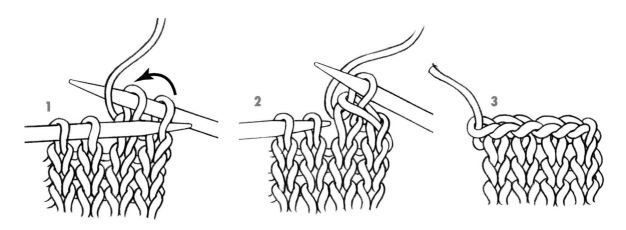

Weaving in ends

Beginning and ending tails are woven directly into the fabric. Use a large-eyed, blunt needle for this process. Weave the strand in and out of a place that isn't too visible, such as along the side or into a seam. Give the piece a little tug and snip the remaining end.

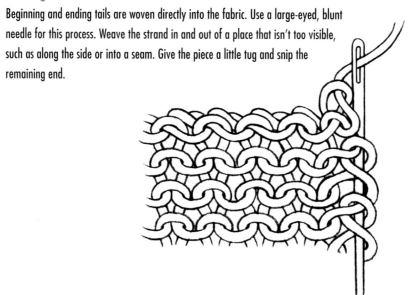

Joining a new ball of yarn

When you use more than one ball of yarn for a project, you will have to tie on a new ball of yarn. Do this at the end of a row, even if you leave a long strand from the old ball of yarn. Tie the new strand loosely onto the old strand, then simply start knitting with the new strand. You can untie the knot when you weave in the end. Keep the old strand out of the way so that you don't use it by mistake.

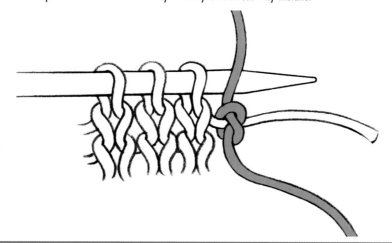

what is gauge?

Measure up in more ways than one

Gauge is a term that is sure to pop up when you start to follow patterns. Gauge is a method of ensuring that your finished knitted or crocheted piece will be the correct size.

You would think that if you just followed the directions, your piece would automatically be sized correctly, but the problem is that everyone knits or crochets with a different tension. This means that the size of a stitch made using exactly the same size needles/hooks and yarn varies from one person to another. Some people even change their tension from project to project.

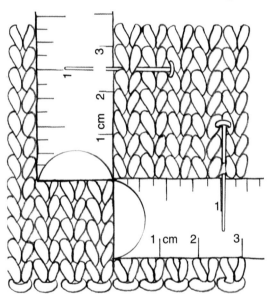

To understand how gauge works, first you need to know how it's presented in a pattern. Usually, gauge will be written something like this: 16 stitches and 20 rows = 4" (10 cm).

Simply put, this means that if you were to make a 4"-square sample based on this pattern (called a gauge swatch), you should aim to create four stitches per inch, or a total of 16 stitches, to yield a sample that is 4" wide. Twenty rows of this stitch should result in a swatch that is 4" long.

As a beginner, it's a good idea to make a gauge swatch before beginning any project. When you make it, use the same yarn, needles or hook, and stitch that you will use for your project. If a pattern does not give the stitch, then you can assume it's done in stockinette stitch (knit on the right side, purl on the wrong side).

After you make the 4" swatch, count the stitches and rows to see if they match the gauge given in your pattern. If, using the example above, you end up with 20 stitches equaling 4", your stitches are too small. This means that if you were to use this stitch to knit a 10" wide scarf, you could end up with one that is only 8" wide. Try using a needle one size larger.

If you end up with only 13 stitches, your stitches are too big. Try going down one needle size, or you could end up with a scarf that's 12" wide.

To measure stitch gauge, lay a tape measure horizontally. Then measure the row gauge vertically. Include half stitches for a more accurate measurement. To make it easier to measure your stitches and rows, use a pencil or another needle to count off each full stitch by inserting the point into the side of each stitch as you count. For quicker measuring, use a stitch gauge tool (see page 32).

The gauge in the pattern assumes you will be using the specified yarn. If you use a different yarn for whatever reason, getting the gauge right is even more important. In this case, you need to make sure your new yarn will work for this pattern. Making a correct gauge swatch is the proof that you need.

THE MANY USES OF SWATCHES

A gauge swatch has many alternative uses, so don't unravel it! Here are just a few ideas:

- Use swatches to see if you like the way a project looks before you begin it.
- Keep them as a record of your project, along with the yarn label.
- Wash them to see how a finished item will launder.
- Save them up and make a patchwork scarf, bag, or pillow.
- Use them to practice adding fringe or embroidery.
- Use them to try out dyes or for shrinking experiments (known as felting, see page 110).

FIRST PERSON DISASTER STORY

Measuring Up

I thought I didn't need to make a gauge swatch until I had an experience that convinced me to always take time for this important step. I was very anxious to begin a sweater for my boyfriend and didn't think that taking the gauge was necessary. To make it worse, I did not even measure the pieces after I had made them. When I put the sweater together, it ended up being big enough to fit two guys. I'm a loose knitter and should have used needles at least two sizes smaller. Boy, was I embarrassed, and all I had to do was take time to make a 4" gauge swatch before I started.

——Rosa M., Buffalo, NY

my first scarf

A great beginner project

Size
4" x 62" without fringe

Materials
- 2 balls of Tahki/Stacy Charles Baby Print
  100% Merino Wool
  3 1/2 oz (100 g) – 60 yds (55 m)
  #42 Denim Print
- Size 19 (15 mm) knitting needles, or size to get gauge
- Large-eyed, blunt needle (for working in ends)
- Crochet hook (size K or larger) to add fringe

Gauge
8 stitches and 12 rows = 4" (10 cm)

Notes
1. Before you begin, cut 32 pieces of yarn 14" long (wrap 32 times lengthwise around a video box and cut one end) for fringe. Set aside.
2. Just before one ball is finished, tie on a new ball of yarn (see page 65).

Scarf
Cast on 8 stitches. Knit every row until there is just enough yarn left to bind off (about 24" or so). Bind off all stitches. Weave in ends.

Fringe
Make 4 fringes along the short ends with 4 strands of yarn in each fringe. Follow fringing instructions on page 105.

fun kid's hat

It's super easy!

Size
Child's medium (16" circumference)

Materials
- 1 ball of Lion Brand Wool-Ease Thick & Quick
  80% Acrylic, 20% Wool
  6 oz (170 g) – 108 yds (98 m)
  #138 Cranberry
- Size 15 (10 mm) knitting needles, or size to get gauge
- Large-eyed, blunt needle (for working in ends)

Gauge
9 stitches and 20 rows = 4" (10 cm)

Hat
Cast on 36 stitches. Knit every row until the piece measures 8".
Bind off all stitches.

Finishing
Fold piece in half widthwise and sew side seam closed (see page
103, on seaming). Sew bind-off edge to close top of hat. Make two
pom-poms (see page 104). Insert the tail of one pom-pom into
the top corner of the hat. Turn hat inside out and use blunt needle
to secure the pom-pom in place. Repeat on other corner. Weave
in ends.

now what do I do?

Answers to common questions

Once I take the band off a skein of yarn, it gets all tangled up. What can I do to prevent this?

Don't take the band off! Try pulling the end of the yarn from the center of the ball or skein while leaving the band intact; this will keep your yarn neat. If the strand isn't visible, insert your thumb and forefinger into the center of the ball and pull out the center strand. You may need to pull out a few yards to get to the end, but don't worry. You will quickly use up any excess as you knit.

I didn't drop a stitch, but I've created a hole somehow and now I have an extra stitch. What did I do wrong?

You probably put a strand of yarn over the needle while working, rather than under. This is actually a type of stitch called a yarn over. You'll learn more about using this stitch as a way of increasing in chapter 6. You can unravel your piece back to the mistake or you can just sew the hole closed. Or take it to an expert, who will often be able to fix it by adjusting the vertical stitches down to it. It will not be very visible on your finished piece. Don't worry too much about small mistakes like these; as you become more experienced, problems like these are less likely to occur.

My friend just wraps the yarn around the needle to cast on the stitches. Can I do the same?

Your friend's method, though it may seem like an easy shortcut, is not a good idea for several reasons. First, by wrapping the yarn around the needle instead of casting on the stitches in the knit cast-on method, you are not creating a good foundation for the rest of your piece. You also will have a hard time knitting the first row, because it will be difficult to insert the needle into the stitches. Start with the cast on shown on page 57, and you'll be better off in the end.

I can never figure out which is the right side. What is a good trick for keeping track so that I know when to knit and when to purl?

Put a safety pin on the knit side. When you turn to that side, you will always know that you must knit the row. "Seeing" your knitting will become second nature with practice.

NOW WHERE DO I GO?

WEB SITES

www.learntoknit.com

www.vogueknitting.com/tech
Click on "Learn to Knit"

www.knitting.about.com
Click on "Learn to Knit"

BOOKS

Hip to Knit: 18 Contemporary Projects for Today's Knitter
By Judith Swartz
Great projects for beginners!

Yarn Girls' Guide to Simple Knits
By Julie Carles and Jordana Jacobs
Larger projects such as sweaters and wraps done in wonderful yarns.

Knitting Pretty
By Kris Percival
Basic techniques and great projects for beginners.

Vogue Knitting Beginner Basics
Edited by Trisha Malcolm
Handy pocket-sized book with good illustrations and projects.

Simple Knits for Sophisticated Knitting: Fast Home Projects from Beautiful Chunky Yarns
By Barbara Albright
Simple, fast-to-make designs created with the beginner in mind.

Chapter 5

USING KNIT AND PURL STITCHES

making ribbing

U p to now you have been knitting complete rows of either knit or
purl stitches. The next step is to combine knit and purl stitches in
the same row. This is called ribbing. If you can knit and purl, you
can easily make ribbing. Ribbing forms a stretchy knitted band that
is good to use for the bottom edge, cuffs, and neckbands of sweaters.
Because it is elastic, ribbing makes it easy to get your sweater over
your head and also keeps it from gaping at the openings.

The most common types of ribbing are knit 1, purl 1 (k1, p1) and knit
2, purl 2 (k2, p2). Knit 1, purl 1 rib is done by knitting 1 stitch and
then purling the next stitch. This kind of ribbing pulls in a bit more
than knit 2, purl 2, but both types are fine for any place you want
ribbing. With knit 2, purl 2 ribbing, you knit 2 and then purl 2.

When you make ribbed fabric, all the knit stitches line up over the
knit stitches and the purl stitches line up over the purl stitches. The
most common problem for beginners is keeping your stitches lined
up. To avoid this, make sure you know the difference between knit
and purl stitches. Watch your stitches as you work them.

When you make a sweater, the ribbed parts are most often done on
knitting needles one or two sizes smaller than those used for the
body. This allows the ribbing to pull in and hold tighter. For
straight ribbing that doesn't pull in, use the same size needles as
used for the body.

RIBBING TIPS

- Cast on and bind off
loosely so that your ribbing
will stay elastic at both the
top and bottom edges.
- Don't feel daunted by ribbing patterns: They're simple to do because they consist of only two rows—one
right side and one wrong
side, repeated over and over.
- Use a safety pin to mark
one side of your piece as the
front before you start ribbing. It will make figuring
out where you are much
easier.
- Measure the number of
stitches for the ribbing
gauge with the piece slightly
stretched.
- Yarns that have more elasticity, such as wool, make
"bouncier" ribbing than yarn
without much elasticity such
as cotton or silk.

TWO SIMPLE RIBBING STITCHES

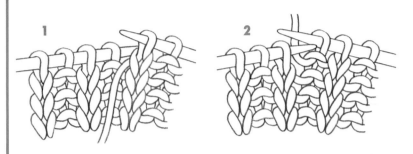

Knit 1, purl 1 ribbing

1. Your pattern will say: "knit 1, purl 1 across the row." After you knit one stitch, bring the yarn to the front, between the needles, so that you will be ready to purl the next stitch.

2. After you finish making a purl stitch, bring the yarn to the back between the needles. Then work a knit stitch.

Continue alternating for as many rows as your pattern requires.

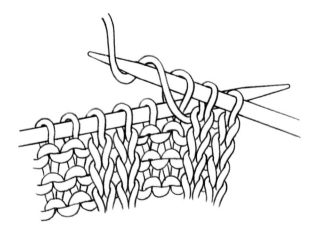

Knit 2, purl 2 ribbing

Knit two stitches and then bring the yarn to the front, between the needles. Purl the next two stitches.

Repeat until you have completed the number of knit 2, purl 2 rows of ribbing required by your pattern.

using ribbing

A versatile stitch

Sometimes ribbing is used for whole projects, but more often it is just a part of the piece. When it is used in this way, ribbing keeps pieces from rolling, or shapes and pulls in certain areas. For example, ribbing on the cuffs of mittens or gloves keeps them in place on your wrist.

Ribbing Uses:

- Hats
- Headbands
- Scarves
- Cowls
- The calf section of socks
- Cuffs on mittens
- Button and buttonhole bands on jackets and cardigans
- Sleeve cuffs and bottom edges of sweaters
- Neckbands on sweaters
- Collars and hoods
- Tube tops
- Allover ribbed sweaters
- Straps on bags
- Blankets

ASK THE EXPERTS

My ribbing pattern calls for an odd number of stitches so that I end with a knit 1. What stitch do I start with on the next row?

On the next row, you would begin with the opposite stitch—purl 1. This second row will end with a purl 1. The use of uneven numbers is to balance the piece. When you make a sweater, this balancing makes it easier to stitch the front and back together, creating a continuous look. When you start your ribbing, read the pattern to see whether it has an even or uneven number of stitches before you begin. If it has an even number, keep in mind you will end with a purl 1 and begin with a knit 1.

My pattern says to make a 1" ribbing on my sweater. If I make the ribbing longer, what will happen?

Longer ribbing pulls in more than shorter ribbing. The current fashion is boxier sweaters, which is the main reason why most sweaters call for short ribbings. If you want to make a longer ribbing, be sure to deduct the extra length from the total number of inches you are supposed to work on the body of your sweater unless you intend to make your sweater longer.

Can I combine any number of knits and purls to make ribbing?

Sure, you can come up with many other rib variations. Try knit 3, purl 3 or knit 4, purl 4 or uneven ribbing such as knit 3, purl 2 or knit 4, purl 2. Such alternate ribbings can be used in place of knit 1, purl 1 or knit 2, purl 2 ribbing. You should be aware, however, that when you have too many knits and purls (such as knit 6, purl 6), ribbing no longer works because it loses its stretchy properties.

a ribbed hat

Using knit 1, purl 1 ribbing

Size

16$^1/_2$" circumference
This hat has lots of stretch and fits any size head.
Make the hat longer if desired.

Materials

- 1 ball of Lion Brand Wool-Ease Thick & Quick
  80% Acrylic, 20% Wool
  6 oz (170 g) – 108 yds (98 m)
  #099 Fisherman
- Size 15 (10 mm) knitting needles, or size to get gauge
- Large-eyed, blunt needle (for seaming and working in ends)

Gauge

10 stitches and 14 rows = 4" (10 cm) in knit 1, purl 1 ribbing

Hat

Cast on 41 stitches.

Row 1 (right side) Knit 1, purl 1 across the row to the last stitch, knit 1.

Row 2 (wrong side) Purl 1, knit 1 across the row to the last stitch, purl 1.

Repeat rows 1 and 2 until piece measures 10". Loosely bind off all stitches.

Finishing

Fold the hat in half and sew along the seam (see page 103). Weave in the ends. Thread a piece of yarn about a yard long. Beginning about 1$^1/_2$" down from the bind-off edge, anchor the thread with a knot. Then go in and out under all the knit stitches around the entire hat. Draw the yarn tight to gather the top. Using the needle, go in and out of the fabric a couple of times where it is gathered to keep it in place, then run the thread into the hat and fasten off inside.

combining knits and purls

**Seed stitch
and ridged stitch
are within your grasp**

When you practiced ribbing, you may have accidentally discovered a stitch known as seed stitch. It is made up of rows of knit 1, purl 1 that alternate and do not stack over each other. To make seed stitch, you would knit 1, purl 1 across the row just as in ribbing. On the next row, instead of working purl 1, knit 1 across the row, you repeat the first row and work knit 1, purl 1. This is a versatile, pebble-like stitch, but unlike ribbing it isn't elastic and won't pull in.

Another easy stitch pattern is made when you combine garter stitch (knit every row) with stockinette stitch (knit 1 row on the right side, purl 1 row on the wrong side). This is called a ridged stitch. (See the pattern for a ridged scarf on page 84.) Unlike ribbing, this fabric doesn't stretch side-to-side, although it does have up-and-down stretch. This stretch makes it great for accessories such as hats and scarves.

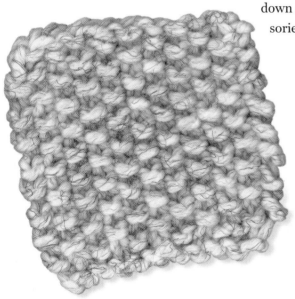

Another way to make a similar fabric is to combine rows of stockinette stitch with another stitch called reverse stockinette stitch (purl 1 row on the right side, knit 1 row on the wrong side). The difference is that garter stitch ridges appear to lie on the stockinette stitch and reverse stockinette stitch rows make a more wavy "hill and valley" effect.

Don't be surprised if you find these two stitch types called by different names. Seed stitch is often called moss stitch or sand stitch. Ridged stitches can be known as garter or reverse stockinette ridges.

FIRST PERSON　　　SUCCESS STORY

Back on Track

When I first started knitting, I could never identify knits and purls or see where I was as I worked my rows. When I started doing pattern stitches, it got more difficult for me. I had a great teacher who took time to help me devise a counting system. I used index cards to keep track of my rows. I made one card for each row and flipped them over as I worked them. She also showed me the difference between the Vs (knits) and bumps (purls). Before long I was able to "read" my knitting. It made all the difference for me.

—Myriam D., Sunnyvale, CA

a ridged scarf

It's just rows
of knits and purls

Size
5" x 60"

Materials
- 2 balls of Tahki/Stacy Charles Baby
  100% Merino Wool
  $3^{1}/_{2}$ oz (100 g) – 60 yds (55 m)
  #22 Grass Green
- Size 17 (12.75 mm) knitting needles, or size to get gauge
- Large-eyed, blunt needle (for working in ends)

Gauge
8 stitches and 13 rows = 4" (10 cm) in ridged stitch

Notes
1. When one ball is finished, tie on a new ball of yarn (see page 65).
2. To balance your scarf, begin and end with 4 knit rows. This means you may have to stop knitting the scarf when you're down to the last 2 or 3 yards of yarn, so you'll have enough to knit these 4 rows.

Scarf
Cast on 10 stitches.
Knit 4 rows.

Pattern begins:
Row 1 Purl.
Row 2 Knit.
Row 3 Purl.
Rows 4–8 Knit.
Repeat these 8 rows until there is about 24" of yarn left. End with row 7 of pattern so that the beginning and end will look the same. Bind off all stitches. Weave in ends.

rolling and nonrolling stitches

Why your fabric curls up

Stitches such as stockinette stitch are not easy to keep flat because the edges curl. There is nothing wrong when this happens, it is simply the property of the stitch. Curling is OK in a long, skinny scarf, but most of the time you want to keep your knit pieces flat.

You don't have to avoid using stockinette stitch, just learn how to counteract the rolling tendency. In a sweater you can add nonrolling stitches, such as ribbing, to the edges. If you are making a scarf or hat, edge it with ribbing or another nonrolling stitch, such as garter or seed stitch. These are also good for the edges of a sweater.

These and other nonrolling stitches are good for projects that you don't want to curl, such as scarves. When you're looking for other stitches that don't curl, try to find one that has a balanced combination of knit and purl stitches. The more it is like stockinette stitch, the more likely that it will roll.

You can also "go with the flow" and allow your pieces to have a natural roll at the edges. This works best on sweaters and accessories such as hats. See the rolled edge sweater on page 120.

WHEN YOUR PIECE ISN'T PERFECT

- Check your work frequently so this doesn't happen to you as often.
- Get some advice from an expert (teacher, friend, or yarn shop owner). Someone with experience can often help you salvage your project.
- Wash it in cold water by hand. Most uneven stitches go away after washing.
- If it's too small or large, find someone whom it fits.
- If you are halfway through a piece and discover a mistake, decide if it is worth ripping or if you can live with the flaw.
- When you really hate your finished piece, rip it out and reuse the yarn for a new project. It happens to all knitters.
- If you make a hole by mistake, sew it together and forget it.
- Most beginners are too critical of their first knitting undertakings. Relax!
- Call a mistake in a pattern stitch a new design element—it just adds to the handmade quality of your piece.

USING EDGE STITCHES

Whether you are making something with a seam (a sweater) or without (a scarf), using edge stitches (known as selvage or selvedge stitches) neatens up your knitting. You can make an edge stitch in a couple of different ways. One really simple way is to knit the first and last stitch of every row, regardless of what the pattern calls for. This edge stitch not only gives you a good place to sew your seam together, it also makes a firm edge.

When making a nonseamed scarf, you may want to add several edge stitches to either side so you'll have a nice flat scarf. An example would be to knit the first and last three stitches on every row. An easy way to keep track of these edge stitches is to knit to the place where you want to do your edge stitches, then place a stitch marker on your knitting needle. Slip the marker onto the other needle when you come to it on the next row. This will remind you to always knit the stitches beyond the marker.

now what do I do?

Answers to common questions

I made a scarf in black using a knit and purl stitch, and the stitches don't show up very well. Why does this happen?

Most stitch patterns have more definition in lighter-colored yarns. Dark shades and variegated yarns make it harder to see stitches. This does not mean that you need to avoid dark or multicolored yarns, just do simpler stitches in these shades and allow the yarn to be the focus of the project. If you are making stitches (such as cables) that you want to show, pick light to medium colors.

How do I change from ribbing to another stitch pattern on the same piece? Do I have to do something special?

You do not need to do anything special to change from one stitch pattern to another. If you begin the lower edge of a hat in ribbing pattern, for example, and want to start a new pattern, just go ahead and start the new stitch pattern on the next row. If, however, you're changing to stockinette stitch, just remember to figure out which side is the outside of the hat first, because you always start stockinette stitch with a knit row on the side that faces out.

What does it mean to "bind off in ribbing"?

This means that instead of creating a ribbed section and then binding it off in knit stitches, such as at the end of a sleeve, you continue ribbing to the very edge of the piece, binding off the ribbed row. The first step in binding off, as described on page 64, is to knit two stitches. When you bind off in ribbing instead, you start out just as if you were working a regular row of ribbing, but then bind off the rib stitches. For example, to bind off knit 1, purl 1 ribbing, you would knit the first stitch, purl the second stitch, and then pull the first stitch over the second stitch. To continue, you would knit the next stitch, bind off, and then purl the next stitch and bind off.

When I go from a knit stitch to a purl stitch when I work ribbing, the stitch ends up loose. How can I correct this problem?

Going between knit and purl stitches on patterns such as ribbing can cause a little difference in your tension. Try to be aware of keeping an even tension and pulling the yarn a little tighter when you complete each stitch. The more you practice ribbing pattern stitches, the less often you will have this problem.

NOW WHERE DO I GO?

WEB SITES

The following sites are good sources of free patterns. Some have helpful technical information.

www.knitting-crochet.com

www.thesmartyarns.com
Click on "Projects"

www.frugalhaus.com
Click on "Patterns"

BOOKS

The Knitting Experience Book 1:
The Knit Stitch
By Sally Melville
A great book full of techniques, inspiration, and projects using only the knit stitch.

The Knitting Experience Book 2:
The Purl Stitch
By Sally Melville
The second in the series, it combines the knit and purl stitches. Full of fashionable patterns.

How to Knit
By Debbie Bliss
Well-known English author Debbie Bliss leads readers through a series of workshops that teach all about knitting. Some parts of the book go beyond beginner skills, but there is great inspiration offered here.

Chapter 6

BEYOND BASIC KNITTING

the ins and outs of loops

Knitting and purling into the back of stitches

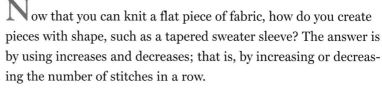

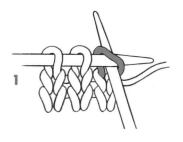

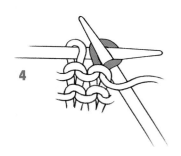

Now that you can knit a flat piece of fabric, how do you create pieces with shape, such as a tapered sweater sleeve? The answer is by using increases and decreases; that is, by increasing or decreasing the number of stitches in a row.

One technique that comes in handy for learning the increases and decreases described in the next few pages is knitting or purling into the back of a stitch. As you know, the normal way to knit or purl is to work through the front of the stitch. (If you are not instructed otherwise, always assume this is the method you should use.)

However, if you insert the needle into the back strand of the stitch, then knit or purl it, you can create a variety of effects. Knitting or purling into the back of the stitch results in twisted stitches, which are sometimes used to make twisted ribbing. This technique can be also found in some patterns that require certain cable stitches.

1. Knitting into the front of a loop
Insert the right needle from front to back into the front strand of the stitch and knit it.

2. Knitting into the back of a loop
Insert the right needle from front to back into the back strand of the stitch and knit it.

3. Purling into the front of a loop
Insert the right needle from right to left into the front strand of the stitch and purl it.

4. Purling into the back of a loop
Insert the right needle from right to left into the back strand of the stitch and purl it. Of the four ways to knit and purl, this takes the most practice.

Slipping a stitch means that you move it from one needle to the other without working it. This technique is frequently used when decreasing and also in certain more advanced stitch patterns. The way you move the stitch from one needle to the other is important. There are two ways: as if you're going to knit and as if you're going to purl. If the pattern doesn't say how to slip the stitch, assume that you should move it as if you're going to purl.

Slipping as if to purl (purlwise)

Insert the right needle into the stitch on the left needle as if you were going to purl it. Move it onto the right needle without working the stitch.

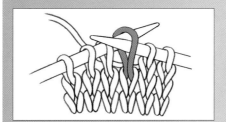

Slipping as if to knit (knitwise)

Insert the right needle into the stitch on the left needle as if you were going to knit it. Move it onto the right needle without working the stitch.

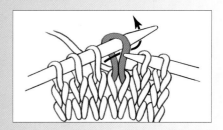

FIRST PERSON SUCCESS STORY

All Twisted Around

I was a self-taught knitter and didn't realize that I was knitting the wrong way. Though I purled the correct way, I would knit by going into the back of the stitch. Then I would wonder why my knitting wasn't smooth and why the stitches didn't look like they did in the pictures in magazines and books. I asked my aunt, who is a more experienced knitter, to observe me to see what I was doing wrong, then she showed me how to knit in the front of the stitch. Such a simple correction made a world of difference! My stockinette stitch is now smooth and flat—and all the twisted stitches are gone.

—Tracie B., Ashford, NC

adding stitches

Learning to shape your knitting adds a whole new level to your knitting experience. As you've just learned, this is done through increasing or decreasing the number of stitches as you go along.

When it comes to increases, there are a number of different techniques. Increases are broken down into two basic categories: increases that are visible and ones that are invisible. Generally you can use either, as even visible increases don't show very much.

When making increases over a number of rows or adding several increases in one row, count your stitches often. This helps you to keep track of how many stitches you have added and how many more are needed. If you forget to add a stitch at a designated spot, don't unravel your piece to correct the error—simply add the forgotten stitch on another row.

Increases are often made at the edges of a piece, where they will be less visible. To keep a smoother edge line, make the increase one or two stitches from the edge and then use selvage stitches for those last two stitches (see page 87).

In a pattern, increases are sometimes spelled out in a section called a stitch glossary. This is usually done if there are special details that you should know (such as an increase that adds more than one stitch). Then again, the pattern may not tell you how to increase, and just say: "Increase one stitch at the beginning and end of the row." You can then work the type of increase that you prefer.

THREE BASIC INCREASES

The main difference between these three increases is how visible they are on knit fabric. Otherwise, they all have the same result: They add a stitch to your piece.

Increase one in stitch (inc 1)

This is the most visible increase, made by using an existing stitch. Also called a bar increase or "knit in front and back of stitch."

1. Knit the stitch by inserting the needle, wrapping the yarn, and pulling through a loop. Now stop! Don't slip the stitch from the left needle.

2. Insert the right needle into the back of the stitch (see "knitting into the back of a loop" on page 92) as shown and knit the loop left on the left needle. You now have two stitches.

Yarn over increase (yo)

This is a slightly visible increase that adds a new stitch.

1. Bring the yarn to the front and lay it over the needle. Knit the next stitch. This forms a loop, or hole, in the piece. (This type of increase is often used to make lacy stitches or buttonholes.) Finish the row according to the pattern.

2. On the next row, when you get to the loop you made on the previous row, purl the loop to add the new stitch to the piece.

Make one increase (M1)

The least visible increase, this is made between two stitches.

1. Put the tip of the left needle under the horizontal bar (the strand between two stitches) and lift the strand onto the left needle.

2. Knit the strand on the left needle through the back of the stitch (see page 92). This is an important step. If you knit it in the front of the stitch, you will create a hole.

Note: It is less common to have a purl make one (PM 1), but you should know how to do it. Pick up the loop just as described in step 1. Now purl the loop through the back of the stitch (see "purling into the back of the loop" on page 92).

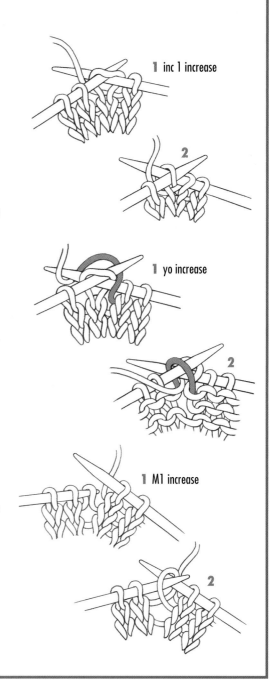

1 inc 1 increase

2

1 yo increase

2

1 M1 increase

2

subtracting stitches

Removing knit stitches

THE SKP DECREASE

There is an outdated form of these decreases called the SKP, which shows up in some older patterns. In this, you slip one stitch purlwise (see page 93), knit the next stitch, then pass (or lift) the slipped stitch over the knit stitch. The ssk decrease looks exactly the same and is considered a modern update to SKP decrease.

Like increases, decreases shape knitting. Decreases can be used in combination with binding off. For example, to shape an armhole, you might bind off a number of stitches and then decrease more stitches on the next few rows. You can't bind off at the end of a row, because it puts the yarn in the wrong place to start a new row. However, you can decrease at the end of the row.

As with increasing, there is more than one way to make a decrease. The main way decreases vary is in terms of how the stitches "lean" when they are decreased. The "lean" factor is somewhat important when making certain types of stitch patterns, such as lace, or when making a special "fully fashioned" armhole where the decreases are used as a decorative effect. For a beginning knitter, the subtlety of stitches leaning to the left or right is not very important. It is more important to know the names of the decreases and how to make them.

Decreases are usually given by name in the pattern. Rarely will a pattern say to "decrease one stitch," although you could find patterns that say "decrease [a number of] stitches evenly across the row." More often, a pattern will say "knit 2 together" or "purl 2 together." Special decreases, such as ones decreasing more than one stitch (called double or triple decreases), will be spelled out in a glossary in the pattern.

NOTE: Decreases can be made a stitch or two from the edge to keep the edge neat.

TWO BASIC TYPES OF DECREASES

Right-leaning or right-slanting decreases

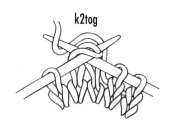

Knit two together (k2tog)
On a knit row, insert the right needle into two stitches. Knit the stitches together. This decreases one stitch.

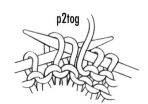

Purl two together (p2tog)
On a purl row, insert the right needle into two stitches. Purl the stitches together. This decreases one stitch.

Left-leaning or left-slanting decreases

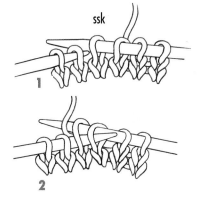

Slip, slip, knit (ssk)
1. On a knit row, slip the next stitch from the left needle to the right just as if you were going to knit it, but don't knit it. Then slip the next one in the same way.
2. Knit the stitches together by inserting your left needle into the front of both stitches as shown.

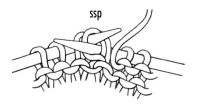

Slip, slip, purl (ssp)
This is a less common decrease. To do this, on a purl row insert the right needle and slip each stitch to the right needle as if you were knitting them. Then put them back on the left needle and purl them through the back loop of the stitch (see page 92).

a bias scarf

Getting the hang of shaping

Size
4" x 72"

Materials
- 1 ball each of Crystal Palace Cotton Chenille
  100% Mercerized Cotton
  $1^{3}/_{4}$ oz (50 g) – 98 yds (88 m)
  #6320 Light Olive (A)
  #5800 Medium Taupe (B)
  #3417 Khaki (C)
  #5137 Brick (D)
- Size 11 (8 mm) knitting needles,
  or size to get gauge
- Large-eyed, blunt needle
  (for working in ends)

Gauge
14 stitches = 4" (10 cm) in garter stitch
(knit every row)

Notes
1. Scarf is worked with two strands of yarn held together and worked as if they were one strand.
2. Count the stitches every few rows to make sure that you have made one increase and one decrease on every other row.
3. Mark the right side of your scarf by placing a safety pin into the fabric. Move the pin closer to your knitting needles each time you begin a new color sequence, so that the pin is always visible.

Scarf
With one strand of A and one strand of B held together, cast on 14 stitches.
Row 1 (right side) Knit 1, knit 1 into the back and front of the stitch (increase 1 stitch), knit to the last three stitches, knit 2 together (decrease 1 stitch), knit 1.
Row 2 (wrong side) Knit all stitches.
Repeat rows 1 and 2 until there are 20 ridges (40 rows).
Drop color A and tie on color C (see joining yarns on page 65). Continue rows 1 and 2 using colors B and C for 20 ridges.
Continue in this way, dropping one strand and attaching a new strand and working 20 ridges as follows:
- C + D
- D + A
- A + B
- B + C
- C + D
- D + A
Loosely bind off all stitches.

Optional fringe
Cut six 13" strands of each of the four colors of yarn. Using three strands of one color at a time, and a size I or J (5.5 or 6 mm) crochet hook, make four fringes (see page 105), one in each color, on each end of the scarf.

blocking your pieces

If your finished piece is fairly even and flat, you can omit any further steps before you sew your seams. If the edges are a little uneven and your knitting could use a little smoothing, some finishing should be done before you sew them together.

Blocking is the process of shaping knitted and crocheted pieces for sewing or simply to give a professional finish to your project. With many of today's yarns, it is not necessary to go to extreme measures to get good results.

How you block is dictated by the kind of yarn used. See the next page to determine which method to use on which kinds of textiles. When in doubt, practice on a swatch before you do anything to your finished pieces.

There are two blocking methods:

Wet blocking Place a large towel onto a clean carpeted floor or cushioned area you can pin into, such as a bed. Wet the whole piece, either by dunking it into water and gently wringing it out, or by using the even easier spray-bottle method and spritzing with water once the piece is in place on the towel. Once it is laid on the towel, use T-pins or straight pins (rustproof) to pin it into place every couple of inches along the outside edges, pulling it to create straight edges. To block without pins, spread out the piece and shape it. Either way, allow the piece to dry completely before moving it. Depending on the type of yarn used, it will usually dry overnight or within 24 hours.

Steaming Use a dampened cloth and steam iron. Place the cloth onto the piece and hold the iron slightly above the cloth to allow the moisture to flatten the seams. The setting used for the iron depends on the fiber in the yarn being steamed.

Read the yarn label care instructions and review the fiber content before you attempt any finishing. Heat is tough on knitted fabric, so be especially careful when steaming man-made fibers.

Wool Wool can take wetting or steaming well, and can easily be molded into shapes. If your finished wool piece is too small, you can alter it somewhat by wetting and pinning it. To steam, use the wool setting on your iron.

Wool blends The higher the percentage of wool, the more likely you can wet or steam your piece as you wish. Steam carefully when using yarns that are more than 50 percent acrylic or some other man-made fiber.

Cotton and cotton blends Light steaming is often all you need for cotton fibers. Cotton does not change its shape when wet. Again, take care with yarns that have a high acrylic content.

Acrylic and man-made fibers While most of these yarns are machine washable and dryable, they don't take well to pressing and steaming. Be careful about using high temperatures on man-made fibers. Direct pressing may melt the fibers or cause them to become limp.

Other animal fibers Treat mohair, alpaca, cashmere, camel hair, lamb's wool, and other animal fibers the same way you would treat wool. Pieces made from longhair fibers, such as mohair, benefit from a little shaking or fluffing in the dryer at an air setting once dry.

Rayon, silk, linen, and other fibers The best thing to do with any of these fibers is to spray them damp, then block if needed. Avoid steaming fibers when you are unsure about the results.

sewing it all up

The big finish

Aside from scarves, most projects have at least one seam. The good news is that you don't have to know much about sewing to seam knits. And because you are using yarn, it's much faster than sewing with thread.

Begin with a large-eyed, blunt needle (see page 32). This kind of needle makes it easy to seam together pieces. Generally you seam with the same yarn you used for the project, unless that yarn is textured, bumpy, or pulls apart easily (such as a loosely spun wool). In such a case, use a coordinating plain yarn for sewing. When working with a thick yarn, you can separate the yarn plies (strands) and sew with one strand of the yarn, rather than the whole thick piece.

What kind of sewing stitch you use depends on the kind of seam you are sewing. The most basic method involves sewing vertical seams on either stockinette or garter stitch pieces, which means joining two pieces together by moving down the rows. It is also helpful to know how to seam two pieces together on the horizontal, or by joining them across the stitches in two rows. This is especially helpful for things such as the shoulders on a sweater.

For best results, line up the two edges side by side with the right sides facing out. You can use a tail of yarn that is left from casting on or binding off. It is not necessary to make a knot, and, in fact, it is better to avoid using any knots. When you begin, run the yarn in and out of an inconspicuous place next to where you are going to begin your seam. Then just start sewing, taking care not to pull out the end.

Seaming on garter stitch (vertical seam)

Line up your two pieces side by side with the right sides facing up and attach the yarn to the lower edge of one piece by weaving it in and out. Insert the needle into the lower edge of the stitch on the opposite side from where the yarn is attached. Pull the yarn through and tighten it a bit. Take the needle and insert it into the upper edge of the same stitch on the other piece and pull the yarn through again. Keep alternating side to side along the entire seam.

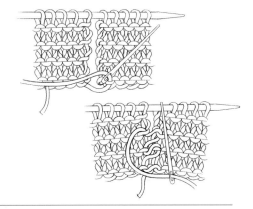

Seaming on stockinette stitch (vertical seam)

Working with the right sides facing you, line up the pieces and attach the yarn to the lower edge of one piece. Put the needle under the horizontal bar between the first two stitches on the other piece. Go back and forth up the seam. On stockinette fabric, work in the center of each edge stitch. When seaming with a thick yarn, work one stitch in from the edge to make the seam less bulky.

Sewing a horizontal seam

Working with the right sides facing you, line up the pieces and attach the yarn. To sew horizontal seams, work on either side of the bind-off rows. Put the needle under one V (one stitch) on the opposite side from where the yarn is attached. Go into the opposite side and go under one V. Continue to go back and forth from side to side along the entire seam.

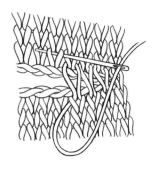

embellishments

Fun little extras

There are a million ways to embellish finished knit and crochet projects. Fringe, tassels, and pom-poms are some of the easiest add-ons you can create, and by varying the length, fullness, and number of embellishments, you can make each of your pieces unique. Some embellishments, such as tassels and pom-poms, you make separately and then attach. Others, like fringe, are created on the piece itself.

You start making most of these add-ons by wrapping the yarn around cardboard, a video box, a book, or any stiff material of the correct size. If you love pom-poms and tassels, you can even purchase a commercial gadget for making them.

Be sure to leave a tail of yarn on pom-poms and tassels for easy attachment. Thread the yarn end through a large-eyed, blunt needle (see page 32), then attach the piece by going in and out of the edge several times. Weave the yarn into the fabric and trim the ends.

Some yarns are good for embellishments, while others are more problematic. The best add-ons are made from yarns that don't unravel or fray. When in doubt, make a sample and attach it to your swatch to see what it looks like before you embellish your piece. You can even make embellishments in a contrasting yarn, or use a couple of different colors.

MAKING ADD-ONS

Pom-poms

There are a couple of ways to make pom-poms. Here is the easiest way:

1. Wind the yarn around a piece of cardboard that is about the same height as the diameter of the pom-pom you want to make. Wrap more than you think you need to make a nice full pom-pom.
2. Gently remove the yarn from the cardboard. Tightly tie a piece of yarn (about 10" long) around the center. Cut both ends of the wrapped yarn.
3. Fluff the pom-pom and trim it with scissors.

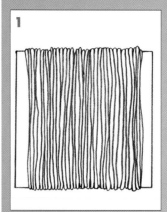

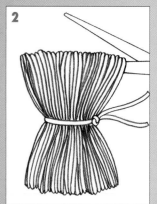

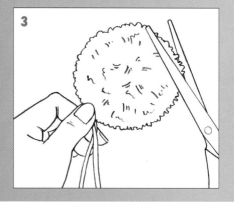

Fringe

1. Wrap the needed strands of yarn (4 to 6 for each fringe) around a firm, rectangular surface, such as a book or video box, and cut along one edge.
2. Fold the yarn in half.
3. Insert a crochet hook through the edge of your piece and pull one folded strand halfway through until you have a loop.
4. Push both ends of the strand through the loop, and then hold the ends together as you pull up to tighten the fringe onto the edge.

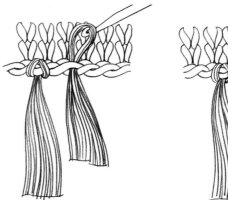

Tassels

1. Cut two strands of yarn about 10" long and put them aside.
2. Follow step #1 for fringe, wrapping 6 to 10 times (depending on the yarn's thickness) for each tassel.
3. Insert the end of one of the cut strands under the top edge of the wrapped yarn. A large-eyed, blunt needle will make this easier to do. Tie it loosely, but don't knot it yet.
4. Cut the bottom edge of the wrapped strands and remove them from the cardboard, then wrap the other 10" piece of yarn around the tassel about an inch from the top.
5. After you have wrapped it enough to secure it, use the needle to push the end into the tassel. Then untie the top strand and attach the tassel as desired.

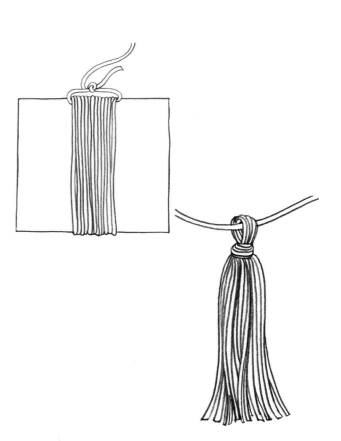

now what do I do?

Answers to common questions

What do I do once I have finished my seam? Do I just knot the yarn and cut it?

To finish a seam it's not necessary to make a knot. All you have to do is to weave the yarn in and out of the fabric a few times. To make it more invisible, go in and out of the inside seam. Snip the yarn, then give the fabric a gentle pull to anchor the yarn. Generally this "tail" will stay in place. If you are using a particularly slippery yarn, however, such as one made from rayon or silk, you might want to weave an inch or so in one direction and then back in the opposite direction for an inch or so, rather than working right on the edge.

My yarn unravels a little when I make fringe, but I don't want to use a different yarn. What should I do?

Don't panic. One trick you can try is tying little knots close to the end of each strand of yarn. The yarn will unravel to the knot, but no further. You can also buy a commercial antifray liquid in sewing, needlecraft, and hobby stores. Dab a little on each strand. The frayed look can also become a design element. In other words, just go with the natural inclination of the yarn.

I decided to try a pattern that calls for increases every few rows to widen the piece, but I'm having trouble remembering when to make the next increase. Help!

A row counter (see page 32) is an ideal way to track your rows. For instance, if you have to make your increase on every fourth row, count each row for three rows, then work the increase on the next row. Either reset your row counter to zero or continue through row seven and make the new increase on row eight. You can also use a pencil and paper to tick off completed rows.

I've made a couple of scarves and hats. Can I make a sweater now?

Once you understand how to increase, decrease, and sew seams, you are certainly ready to make a sweater. Choose a simple pattern for your first sweater project, and use thicker yarn so that you can complete your garment faster and see your stitches clearly. Be sure to check your gauge by making a gauge swatch before you begin. Measure often as you work. Before you know it, you'll have a sweater about which you can proudly say, "I made it myself!"

I want to make a lace scarf. The pattern calls for a number of increases and decreases in one row, though the total number of stitches does not change. Why does this happen?

Lace patterns in knitting are made by making holes (usually by increasing using yarn over stitches). When you make an increase, your knitting will get wider. To prevent this from happening, a decrease is placed in the pattern. If you have a number of increases, each should have a corresponding decrease. This keeps the number of stitches even as you knit. Some lace patterns are quite easy, so once you have learned how to make increases and decreases you should be able to master one of these patterns.

NOW WHERE DO I GO?

WEB SITES

www.kid-craft-central.com/ pom-poms.html
More pom-pom instructions.

www.straw.com/cpy/patterns
Click on "Cocoon Wrap Scarf"
Free pattern for a bias knit scarf.

BOOKS

Knitting from Kids Can Do It Press
By Judy Ann Sadler
This 40-page book from www.kidscanpress.com has great illustrations and many easy projects.

Finishing Techniques for Hand Knitters
By Jane Crowfoot
Everything you need to know about finishing garments and making embellishments, as well as lots of good basic knitting techniques. Many full-color photographs.

Knitting for the First Time
By Vanessa-Ann
Good illustrations of basic and more advanced techniques, plus many projects.

Chapter 7

EXPANDING YOUR KNITTING SKILLS

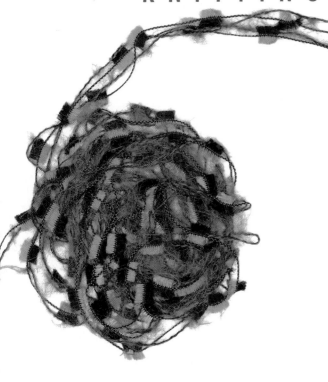

the art of felting

Turning knitting into a felted bag

One of the fun things you can do with knitted material is turn it into felt—a kind of dense, nearly waterproof fabric that's great for hats, mittens, and bags. And believe it or not, felting is pretty easy to do.

All you really need to do is toss a knitted item in a washing machine, then agitate it in hot water with other garments. This causes the knitted fabric to shrink and the individual yarn fibers to "felt," or meld together and form a solid, fuzzy material.

It's important to wash your project with items that won't shed onto the felted piece. Stay away from terrycloth towels, for example, and instead use well-worn towels or denim jeans.

The best yarns to use for felting are animal fibers such as wool, alpaca, and mohair, which felt easily. If you are unsure about the felting properties of a yarn, make a swatch and wash it first. Also, make sure that your yarns are colorfast before you use them in a felting project. This is especially important with high contrast colors such as red and white.

Felting is not an exact science, and exact sizing isn't always possible. For this reason, it's best used on smaller items like bags and accessories. And if you're not sure if an item has shrunk and felted enough, remember that it's better to end up with a piece that's a little bit too big than one that's too small, because there is no way to "unfelt" it.

Let your creativity run wild with felting! From hats and bags to mittens and toys, there's really no limit to what you can do with this craft.

A QUICK FELTED BAG

Size

Before felting: 10" x 12"
After felting: 9" x 10"

Materials

- 1 ball each of Reynolds Lopi 100% Wool
  $3^{1}/_{2}$ oz (100 g) – 110 yds (100 m)
  #005 Dark Charcoal
  #212 Apple
- Size 11 (8 mm) knitting needles,
  or size to get gauge
- One 1" button
- Large-eyed, blunt needle (for seaming)

Gauge

12 stitches and 16 rows = 4" (10 cm) in stockinette
stitch (knit on right side, purl on wrong side)

Notes

Bag is made in one piece. It is folded in half once
completed.

Bag

With Dark Charcoal, cast on 60 stitches and knit 7
rows. Join Apple and work in stockinette stitch (knit
right side rows and purl wrong side rows). Continue
until Apple measures 10". Join Dark Charcoal and
knit 7 rows. Bind off all stitches.

Strap

With two strands of Dark Charcoal, cast on 64
stitches.
Next Row Bind off all stitches.

Finishing

Fold the bag in half lengthwise and sew side seam
using Apple (see page 103 on seaming). Sew bottom
of bag with Dark Charcoal. Place strap ends inside
each side of the bag, about 1" from the top. Sew
securely.

Felting

Put the bag in a washing machine on a hot
wash/cold rinse cycle along with some garments to
agitate. Add detergent and wash. Check the bag
throughout the cycle to see how much felting has
taken place. When the right size is achieved, rinse
and spin. Lie flat to dry. If the piece has not felted
enough, place it in a dryer for a short time. The fabric should be firm, fuzzy, and compressed when felting is complete.

Button

Sew the button to the top edge of one side of the
bag, about 1" from the top. Cut two 6" pieces of
Dark Charcoal and one 6" piece of
Apple. Tie a knot and braid the
three pieces. Tie a knot in the
remaining end. Trim the
ends. Fold the braided piece
so it makes a loop, then
sew it inside the edge of
the bag, opposite the
button, to make a
button loop.

a cozy baby blanket

Bright diagonal squares make this stand out

Size
Finished throw: 30" x 50"
One square: 10" x 10"

Notes on blanket
This blanket, made of 15 knitted squares, is sized for a child. For a smaller infant/stroller blanket, use three skeins of color B, not four, and make only 12 squares.

Materials
- 4 skeins each of Lion Brand Homespun
  98% Acrylic, 2% Polyester
  6 oz (170 g) – 185 yds (167 m)
  #372 Sunshine State (A)
  #317 Pacifica (B)
- Size 11 (8 mm) knitting needles,
  or size to get gauge
- Large-eyed, blunt needle (for seaming)

Gauge
12 stitches = 4" (10 cm) in garter stitch (knit every row)

Notes on squares
Squares are made diagonally, beginning with 4 stitches and working to the full width, then decreasing back to 4 stitches.

Increase and decrease stitches
Yarn over – Increases 1 stitch
Knit 2 together – Decreases 1 stitch

Square
Cast on 4 stitches.
Row 1 Knit the 4 stitches.
Row 2 Knit 2, yarn over, knit to end.
Repeat row 2 until you have 40 stitches on the needle.
Next row Knit 1, knit 2 together, yarn over, knit 2 together, knit to end.
Repeat last row until 5 stitches remain.
Last row Knit 1, knit 2 together, knit 2.
Bind off the remaining 4 stitches.

Blanket
Make 7 squares of color A and 8 squares of color B—15 squares total. For a smaller blanket, make 6 squares of color A and 6 squares of color B—12 squares total. Sew the squares together, alternating A and B squares. Smaller blanket is 3 squares wide and 4 squares long; larger blanket is 3 squares wide and 5 squares long. (See page 103 on seaming.) Weave in ends.

sizing projects

One of the great perks of learning to knit or crochet is that with a little practice you'll soon be able to make one-of-a-kind garments that fit perfectly.

Making something that fits takes a little time when you start your project, but is well worth it in the end. If you're making a sweater for yourself, first review the suggested measurements in your pattern. You will find these measurements on the flat diagrams (schematics) that come with most patterns.

The most important measurements are width (finished chest/bust), overall length, and sleeve length. Take these measurements yourself or ask someone to help you. An easy shortcut is to use the measurements from a sweater that fits you well. Then compare the measurements you've taken to the finished measurements in the pattern to figure out which size sweater you should knit.

Keep in mind that all sweaters have a certain amount of ease—the difference between your actual measurements and the measurements of the finished garment. Look at the photograph of the finished garment to get a general idea of how much ease it has. If the fit shown in the pattern seems comfortable to you, then you don't need to make any adjustments.

If you'd prefer a sweater with more ease, just make the next size up. It's also easy to adjust the body length if you prefer a longer or shorter sweater. This is usually done in the lower portion of the piece, before you do any armhole shaping. For example, if you want to make your sweater 2" shorter, just eliminate 2" from the total inches you are supposed to knit from the bottom edge to the underarm.

The more you veer away from the actual pattern measurements, the more complex will be the adjustments you will need to make. Ask a seasoned knitter for help, or experiment. You'll get the hang of it eventually!

- The fit of knitted and crocheted garments is often more relaxed than the fit of other clothes, because most yarns have a good deal of give.
- Avoid making tight-fitting lower edges on sweaters. They tend to be uncomfortable and unflattering.
- When making a unisex design, remember that men's sweaters should not be too long. Just a few inches below the waist is ideal.
- Baby sweaters should have an easy-access opening for the head. A few options are button bands along the shoulders, a V-neck, or back or front plackets.
- Children grow quickly, so size their sweaters generously. Longer sleeves can always be rolled for the first season.
- Baby and children's sizing is often given in ages. Check with the parents before you begin. Your darling 13-month-old niece may actually wear a 24-month size.
- When making sweaters for other people, either take their measurements or ask them to measure their favorite sweater.
- Keep a notebook with the sizes of people for whom you're likely to make garments.

FIRST PERSON SUCCESS STORY

Making It My Own

I am an average-height gal, but I'm ample in the hip department. When I first started knitting, I didn't know how to read the diagrams and finished measurements in knitting patterns. My first few sweaters were too long or too short, or the sleeves came down below my knuckles. None of them were flattering for my figure type. Finally I took a class in fitting a sweater. It made me realize that I was in control of my knitting! Now I make sweaters that do not end at the widest point of my hips (very unflattering for me) or have overly tight ribbing. I've also learned to alter sleeves. "Create a great-fitting sweater every time" is my new mantra.

—Gena S., Anchorage, AL

adding colors

Stripes and more

Once you know how to knit with one color, the obvious next step is to work with more than one color in the same project. There are a number of ways to combine colors, and some are quite simple for beginning knitters to master.

In the following directions, assume you are doing stockinette stitch (knitting on the right side, purling on the wrong side).

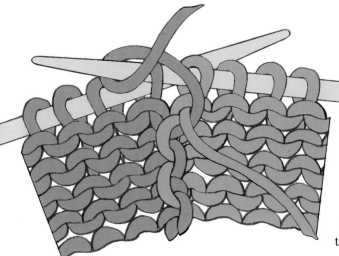

Do the twist: Drop the old color and bring the new color up under the old color—this "locks" the colors into place. Then purl the next stitch using the new color.

Stripes

Making stripes is probably the easiest way to introduce more colors into your piece. When you want to work a new stripe, just tie on the new color before you begin the row. In knitting, you usually make an even number of rows for a stripe, for the simple reason that you will then always change colors on the same edge of your piece.

Stranding

Another way to use color is to work a pattern that has two or more colors in the same row. In stranding, you carry both yarns along the back of the piece as you work and change as directed in the pattern. This technique is used in Fair Isle, a multicolor patterning technique that originated in the Shetland Islands. It works best if there are only a few stitches (two to five) between color changes.

Intarsia

This is also a multicolor technique in which more than one color is used in a row, but in intarsia, there are more stitches between color changes. Unlike in stranding, the yarn you're not knitting with is not carried along the back of the piece; instead, you just drop the old color and start with the new color. To avoid holes where the colors meet, you need to twist the yarns together on the wrong (purl) side of your knitting (see illustration).

ASK THE EXPERTS

I was making stripes on a scarf and I got these funny-looking "ticks" along the row where I changed colors. What did I do wrong?

These "ticks" or "blips" are a natural occurrence between two different colored rows. If you don't want this "ticking" to show on your finished piece, change colors on knit rows only. Then the blips will appear only on the purl side (wrong side) of your piece. You can also make them a design element by working in garter stitch (knitting every row), or by always changing colors on the purl rows.

I am making a two-color striped scarf. Do I have to cut the yarn after each stripe?

No. If, for example, you are making four-row stripes, simply drop the first color and work the stripe in the second color. To begin working another stripe in the first color, pick it up from the edge and start knitting with it again. As you start the first stitch in the new color, don't pull too tightly; just let the strand fall into place naturally, and it will be pulled neatly into the new edge stitches.

My first attempt at working with two colors in a row was a big disappointment. My knit fabric pulled in and got lumpy. How can I keep this from happening next time?

No need to fret—what happened is that you pulled the strand of the new color too tight when you changed from one color to another. When you carry yarn on the back of your knitting, you need to keep this strand loose and even. When you drop one color and bring up the other one, be sure not to draw it too tightly across the back of your knitting. If you think you might be working too tightly, lay the piece flat after a few rows. If it pulls in, just rip out your rows and try again. With a little experience, this problem will soon disappear.

a striped baby vest

A quick gift idea

Size
18 months (2 years, 4 years)

Finished measurements
Chest 24" (28", 30")
Length 10" (12", 14")

Materials
- 1 (1, 2) balls of Lion Brand Magic Stripes
  75% Superwash Wool, 25% Nylon
  3½ oz (100 g) – 330 yds (300 m)
  #200 Jelly Bean Stripe
- Size 9 (5.5 mm) knitting needles,
  or size to get gauge
- Large-eyed, blunt needle (for seaming)

Gauge
16 stitches and 30 rows = 4" (10 cm) in garter
stitch (knit every row) using 2 strands of yarn

Notes
1. When using one ball, work with the inside
strand and outside strand of the ball of yarn
held together throughout the project. You can
also divide the ball into two balls and work
with a strand from each ball.
2. Numbers for 18-month size are given first;
2- and 4-year sizes are given in parentheses.

Front and back (make two identical pieces)
Holding two strands of yarn together, cast on
48 (56, 60) stitches.
Knit every row until the piece measures
6" (7", 8").

Armhole shaping
Bind off 8 stitches at beginning of next two
rows—40 (48, 52) stitches remain.

Continue to knit until armhole is 2½" (3",
3½") deep.

Next row Knit 8 (10, 12) stitches. Slip remaining stitches onto a holder. Turn piece, and knit
back over 8 (10, 12) stitches. Continue to knit
these stitches until armhole measures 4" (5",
6") deep. Bind off 8 (10, 12) stitches.

Slip stitches from holder back onto the needle.
Reattach yarn at first stitch on needle and bind
off the center 16 (20, 20) stitches. Knit last 8
(10, 12) stitches.

Continue to knit remaining stitches on this side
until it is the same size as the other side. Bind
off 8 (10, 12) stitches.

Finishing
Sew side seams and shoulder seams (see page
103 on seaming). Weave in ends.

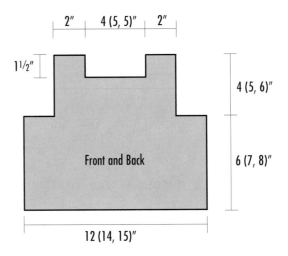

2" 4 (5, 5)" 2"

1½"

4 (5, 6)"

Front and Back

6 (7, 8)"

12 (14, 15)"

my first sweater

An updated classic pullover

Size
Adult S (M, L, XL) (Shown below in size S on a boy; this size is also good for a small woman.)

Finished measurements
Bust 38" (42", 46", 50")
Length 22" (24", 25 1/2", 26")

Materials
- 4 (5, 5, 6) balls of Tahki/Stacy Charles Donegal Tweed, 100% Wool
  3 1/2 oz (100 g) – 330 yds (300 m) #899 Denim
- 1 ball of #892 Celery for trim
- Size 9 (5.5 mm) knitting needles,
  or size to get gauge
- 4 medium-sized stitch holders (see page 33)
- Large-eyed, blunt needle (for seaming)

Gauge
16 stitches and 22 rows = 4" (10 cm) in stockinette stitch (knit on right side, purl on wrong)

Notes
1. Numbers for size S are given first. Sizes M, L, and XL are given in parentheses. For ease in working, circle numbers that relate to your size.
2. Contrasting edging in Celery rolls naturally.
3. Edging rolls up, so sew this part of seams with wrong side out. Includes neckband seam.

Front and Back (make two identical pieces)
With Celery yarn, cast on 76 (84, 92, 100) stitches. Work in stockinette stitch for 1", ending with a purl row. Change to Denim yarn and continue until piece measures 12" (13", 14", 15") from beginning, ending with a purl row.

Armhole shaping
Bind off 1 (2, 3, 4) stitch(es) at the beginning of the next two rows—74 (80, 86, 92) stitches remain.
Decrease row (right side) Knit 1, ssk (see page 97), knit to last 3 stitches, knit 2 together (see page 97), knit 1.
Next row Purl all stitches. Repeat last two rows 24 (26, 27, 28) more times—24 (26, 30, 34) stitches remain. Slip stitches off needle onto a stitch holder.

Sleeves (make two identical pieces)
With Celery yarn, cast on 30 (32, 36, 38) stitches. Work in stockinette stitch for 1", ending with a purl row. Change to Denim yarn and begin increasing 1 stitch on each side every fourth row for a total of 22 times—74 (76, 80, 82) stitches remain. Work even (meaning work without further increases) until the sleeve measures 18" from beginning, ending with a purl row.

Sleeve cap shaping

Bind off 1 (2, 3, 4) stitch(es) at beginning of the next two rows—72 (72, 74, 74) stitches remain.

Next row (right side) Knit 1, ssk, knit to last 3 stitches, knit 2 together, knit 1.

Next row Purl all stitches. Repeat last two rows until 10 (12, 12, 14) stitches remain. Place all stitches on holders.

At this stage, you will have four pieces: one sweater front, one sweater back, and two sleeves. Stitches at the top edges of all pieces should be on stitch holders (see illustration).

Finishing

Use Denim for finishing. With right side facing you, pin armhole edge of one sleeve to armhole on front sweater piece. Sew armhole seam. Pin remaining armhole edge to armhole on back body piece and sew seam—three pieces are now joined. Repeat for other sleeve, but leave last armhole seam open until neckband is worked.

Neckband

With right side facing you and with Celery yarn, knit the stitches off the stitch holder and onto your knitting needle in the following order: one sleeve, front or back piece, other sleeve, remaining back or front piece. There will be 68 (76, 84, 96) stitches on the needle.

Next row Purl, decreasing 8 (8, 10, 10) stitches by purling 2 stitches together evenly along band—60 (68, 74, 86) stitches remain.

Continue to work in stockinette stitch until neckband measures 1$\frac{1}{2}$". Bind off all stitches loosely.

Sew remaining armhole seam and neckband edge.

Sew sweater side seams and long sleeve seams.

Weave in ends. Steam seams with a pressing cloth and iron to flatten and neaten them.

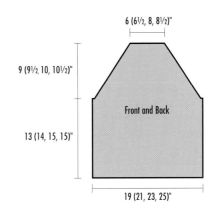

6 (6$\frac{1}{2}$, 8, 8$\frac{1}{2}$)"

9 (9$\frac{1}{2}$, 10, 10$\frac{1}{2}$)"

Front and Back

13 (14, 15, 15)"

19 (21, 23, 25)"

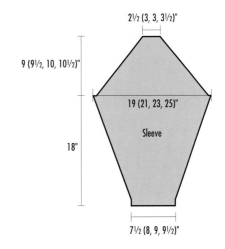

2$\frac{1}{2}$ (3, 3, 3$\frac{1}{2}$)"

9 (9$\frac{1}{2}$, 10, 10$\frac{1}{2}$)"

19 (21, 23, 25)"

Sleeve

18"

7$\frac{1}{2}$ (8, 9, 9$\frac{1}{2}$)"

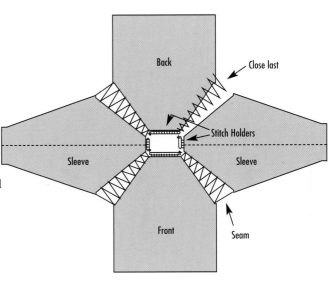

Back

Close last

Stitch Holders

Sleeve

Sleeve

Front

Seam

picking up stitches

A great finish

In the sweater pattern on page 120, you used stitch holders to secure unfinished stitches at the neck edge until you were ready to knit them. Using a similar technique—picking up finished stitches—you can add neckbands and button bands to finished sweaters.

"Picking up stitches" basically means adding a new knitted section that starts with the edge stitches of a finished garment. Neckbands and button bands are often added on after you complete a piece to add stability, and are often done with a smaller needle to make this fabric firmer and denser than the body of the sweater.

How you pick up stitches varies depending on where you pick up the stitches—along horizontal, vertical, or curved edges. On a horizontal edge, pick up each edge stitch along the row. On a vertical edge, the pickup is actually done into rows rather than stitches. And because the gauge is not the same for stitches and rows, you pick up fewer stitches along a vertical edge. Every three or four stitches, skip a row and make the next pickup into the row above. On curved edges, because the stitches are not as defined as on horizontal and vertical edges, just try to pick up as evenly as possible.

The aim is to make an edging that will lie flat. It should not pull in (too few stitches) or be too floppy (too many stitches). This takes a little practice, but once you get the hang of the technique, you'll wonder how you ever did without it!

When you are picking up stitches, this is also a good time to tighten up loose stitches or correct any unevenness in your piece. Loose stitches generally occur more often along curved edges at necklines, and create small holes in the fabric. When you insert the needle to pull up a stitch, close up any holes near the edge by inserting the needle below the hole and pulling through the picked-up stitch.

These illustrations are shown on the knit side of stockinette stitch fabric. The same methods apply to all stitches.

Picking up stitches on a horizontal edge

This is the easiest way to pick up stitches, so you might want to practice this method first.

1. Hold the yarn in back of the piece. Insert the needle through the V of the first stitch (just below the bound-off edge).

2. Place the yarn over the needle just as you would if you were knitting and draw up a loop. Leave a tail of yarn about 6" to 8" long. You may want to hold the tail for a stitch or two so that the stitches do not pull out.

3. Continue to add one stitch for each stitch along the piece. When that's done, you are ready to work your band, using whatever stitch the pattern calls for.

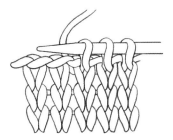

Picking up stitches on a vertical edge

The most common use for this type of pickup is button bands on cardigans.

1. Begin just as you would for a horizontal pickup, but work just inside the first stitch, rather than at the bound-off edge. Instead of inserting the needle into a stitch, go into the strand between the rows.

2. Pick up for approximately three rows and then skip one row. Continue to pick up stitches along the edge as instructed in your pattern.

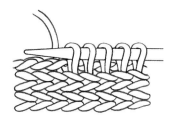

Picking up stitches on a curved edge

1. Necklines are the area where you are most often required to pick up stitches on a curve. Insert the needle and pull up a stitch just as you would do on a horizontal or vertical edge. Be sure to insert the needle into an area that has been bound off, or inside an edge stitch.

2. Continue to pick up stitches along the curve.

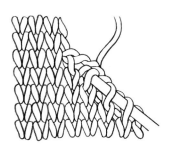

cables

This classic stitch is easier than it looks

If you really want to wow your friends, tell them you can knit cables! These impressive-looking stitches are so simple that even a beginner can make them. Your one big challenge is keeping track of the rows where you have to twist the cables. This is easy to do if you use a row counter or write down the rows as you work them.

Cables are made simply by knitting a number of stitches out of order. This means that when you come to the cable twist row in a pattern, you might be told to skip the next four stitches, jump ahead and knit the next four stitches, then go back and knit the four skipped stitches. Rearranging the stitches this way gives them that distinctive ropelike appearance.

To rearrange the stitches, you will need a cable needle (abbreviated "cn" in patterns) or a double-pointed needle (see page 28). A cable needle allows you to set aside the stitches of the cable so you can jump forward and knit the next set of stitches. Then you can knit the skipped stitches back into the piece directly off the cable needle.

One major variable in cables is the number of stitches used. Most are made using an even number of stitches; four-, six-, and eight-stitch cables are very common. The even number helps to divide the stitches up evenly.

Cables are not twisted on every row, but rather at set intervals; for example, every fourth row might be a turning row. The more frequent the turning rows, the tighter the cable will twist. The number of regular rows between turning rows often correlates with the number of stitches in the cable. For example, a four-stitch cable will likely have four rows between twists.

If you look closely at a cabled sweater, you will notice that the cables twist either to the left or to the right. The direction they twist depends on whether you hold the skipped stitches to the front or back of the piece when making the cable. Using left or right cables is usually just the designer's preference, although sometimes both are used on either side of the same piece for symmetry.

The cables described here are each known by two different names; in patterns, they may be labeled either way. In these directions, they are made with six stitches and the cable twist row is every sixth row. You can use the same technique when working cables with more or fewer stitches.

Cables are most often made in stockinette stitch (knit on right side, purl on wrong side) to give them dimension, and the stitches on either side of the cable are usually done in reverse stockinette stitch (purl on right side, knit on wrong side). Cables are twisted on right-side rows only.

Left (front) cables

1. Work the required number of stitches to the cable group in a cable twist row. Move the first three stitches of the cable onto the cable needle without twisting them. Hold this needle **in front** of your knitting.

2. Jump ahead and knit the next three stitches in the piece.

3. Go back to the first stitch on the cable needle and, using the cable needle like a knitting needle, knit the three stitches on it in this order: first, second, and third. Continue with the rest of the row.

4. Knit the next five rows normally until you come to the next cable twist row. You will start to see the cable pattern develop gradually.

Right (back) cables

1. Work the required number of stitches to the cable group in a cable twist row. Move the first three stitches of the cable onto the cable needle without twisting them. Hold this needle **in back** of your knitting.

2. Jump ahead and knit the next three stitches in the piece.

3. Go back to the first stitch on the cable needle and, using the cable needle like a knitting needle, knit the three stitches on it in this order: first, second, and third. Continue with the rest of the row.

4. Knit the next five rows normally until you come to the next cable twist row. You will start to see the cable pattern develop gradually. Continue with the rest of the row.

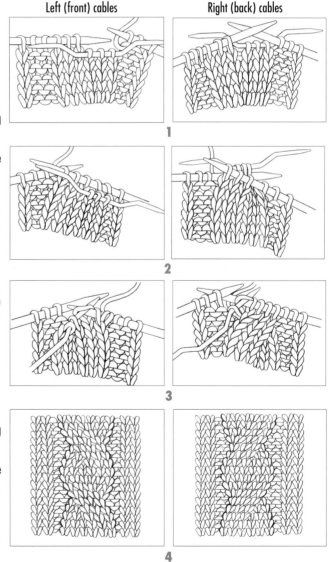

Left (front) cables   Right (back) cables

1

2

3

4

a cabled scarf

You'll finish this in a flash

Size
7" x 36" (without fringe)

Materials
- 1 ball of Lion Brand Wool-Ease Chunky
  86% Acrylic, 10% Wool, 4% Rayon
  5 oz (140 g) – 153 yds (140 m)
  #402 Wheat
- Size 11 (8 mm) knitting needles,
  or size to get gauge
- Cable needle
- Stitch markers

Gauge
10 stitches and 16 rows = 4" (10 cm) in stockinette stitch (but don't worry too much about gauge for this one—scarf sizes don't have to be exact)

Notes
1. Before you begin your scarf, cut 32 strands of yarn by wrapping the yarn lengthwise around a video box.

2. When you have finished making your scarf, instead of weaving the yarn tails, just add them to a fringe.

Cable pattern (worked over 8 stitches)
Slip 4 stitches to a cable needle and hold the stitches in back of the piece, knit the next 4 stitches, then knit 4 stitches from the cable needle—a cable is completed.

Scarf
Cast on 24 stitches. Knit 3 rows.

Note: For ease in working, place markers before and after the center knit 8 stitches. This is where you will make your cable. Slip the markers from the left needle to the right needle when you come to them.

Row 1 (right side) Knit 4, purl 4, knit 8, purl 4, knit 4.

Row 2 (wrong side) Knit 8, purl 8, knit 8.

Row 3 (cable row) Knit 4, purl 4, slip marker, make the cable over the next 8 stitches (follow the cable pattern), slip marker, purl 4, knit 4.

Row 4 Knit 8, purl 8, knit 8.

Rows 5–8 Repeat rows 1 and 2 twice.

Repeat the last 8 rows until the scarf measures 35", ending with a row 8.

Knit 4 rows. Bind off all stitches.

Fringe
Make 4 fringes along both short ends of the scarf, using 4 strands of yarn for each fringe (see page 105 on fringe).

now what do I do?

Answers to common questions

When making a sweater, why do you make the back first?

The front is more visible when you wear a sweater, so if you make the back first, you have time to perfect your technique. When you make a sweater, always measure your pieces as you go along to make sure they are the right size before you move on. To check the size, finish a row, lay the piece on a flat surface, and measure across it with a tape measure. If you have too many stitches bunched on your needle to spread the piece out flat, work half a row and lay down the piece, then take the measurement across the finished rows of the piece.

What does it mean when the pattern says "pick up and knit" the edge stitches to make a neckband? Is this the same as just picking up stitches?

No. "Pick up and knit" means that you need to wrap the yarn around the needle once (just as if you were knitting), rather than just pulling up a loop from the fabric. This method of picking up stitches makes an even, durable edge. Even if your pattern just says to pick up stitches along an edge, for the neatest edging, use the "pick up and knit" technique.

Even though I followed the pattern very carefully, my sweater is too short! What do I do now?

Don't be too hard on yourself—making a sweater too long or too short happens even to the best knitters, and you can probably still fix it. There are three stages at which length adjustments can be made; you can probably use the third technique described below to add some inches to your finished sweater.

1. To add inches at the beginning, before you even begin to knit: Carefully check the pattern's finished measurements to be sure that this is the length you want. This is the best time and the easiest way to make changes to your pattern.

2. To add inches after you have made your pieces: Pin or baste the sweater together, then try it on. If it's too short, you will need to add length to the section below the armhole. To do this, you'll need to rip out the front and back pieces from the neck edge down to where the armhole shaping ends, then add extra rows to the body before reknitting the armhole section. Note that this will require more yarn, so you need to make sure you have enough before you start.

3. To add inches after your sweater is completely finished: Pick up along the lower edge and add a few inches. You may have to add length to the front and the back separately, then sew the side seams. Remember to bind off the new addition very loosely, so that the lower edge will be easy to get on and off. This is a more drastic measure, as it is not so easy to make a neat picked up area, and the new stitches will have to be worked in the opposite direction.

My sweater pattern has a chart instead of written instructions for the cable stitch pattern. How do charts work?

Charts are a type of shorthand, or visual representation, of a stitch pattern. In a chart, one block equals one stitch. A knit stitch is usually represented by a single vertical line. A stitch key that defines each stitch symbol accompanies these charts. If your pattern has both written instructions and a chart, you don't have to use the chart. But magazines and books are increasingly using charts, so it's helpful to become acquainted with them. A good way to get used to charts is to follow the written instructions, but also refer to the chart as you knit.

NOW WHERE DO I GO?

WEB SITES

www.yarnstandards.com
Good sizing charts for women, men, children, and babies.

www.dummies.com/WileyCDA
Do a search under "cables" to find an article with some great cablemaking advice.

www.woolworks.org/patterns.html
Free knitting patterns.

BOOKS

Big Book of Knitting
By Katharina Buss
A 240-page volume full of stitch patterns and techniques, with good information for beginners and much more for those with some experience.

Felted Knits
By Beverly Galeskas
If you liked the felted bag project, this is the book for you. It's full of felting tips, plus great projects like slippers, mittens, pillows, and more bags.

Knit One, Felt Too
By Kathleen Taylor
A book with 25 easy-to-knit felting projects, along with helpful felting advice.

Stitch 'N Bitch: The Knitter's Handbook
By Debbie Stoller
A hip book with lots of fun projects and good basic techniques, done in a quirky, fun way.

Chapter 8

CROCHET BASICS

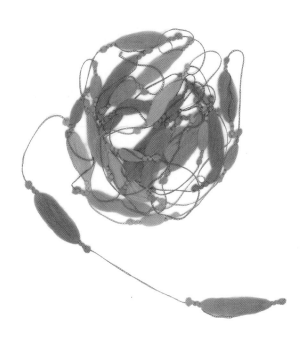

hook holds

Getting comfortable with your hook

Unlike knitting, crocheting requires only one tool—a hook. Since you are using only one implement, you might find crocheting slightly easier. Pick up the hook with your right hand and see how it feels. Even if you are left-handed, you can crochet holding the hook in your right hand. And don't worry—both left- and right-handers feel awkward at first.

There are two basic "holds." Try out either one or both to see what feels the most comfortable to you. In the first one, you hold the hook as you would a pencil. To do this, grasp the hook with your thumb and index finger and allow the hook's end to rest in the space where your thumb joins your hand. In the knife method, you hold the hook with your thumb and index finger, but the end of the hook is held under your hand, as you might hold a knife. If you find another variation for holding, that is perfectly fine. You should do what feels best. It's only important that you can easily make the stitches.

This is a two-handed process. Your left hand is used to hold the yarn and the stitches. As you make crocheted fabric, both hands work together to keep the yarn and the stitches moving along.

Knife hold

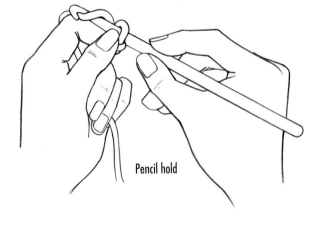

Pencil hold

MAKING A SLIPKNOT

1. Pull about 8" of yarn from your ball or skein. This is the yarn "tail." Create a loop in the middle of the strand, and place it on top of the tail.

2. Holding the loop and the tail together in one hand, use the hook to pull the tail strand up through the loop. Pull both ends of the yarn to tighten the slipknot onto the hook.

MAKING A CROCHET CHAIN (abbreviated as ch)

1. Hold the hook in your right hand and loop the yarn from the ball over your left finger. At the same time, hold the end of the slipknot between your thumb and third finger. Wrap the yarn over the hook and use the hook to draw the yarn through the loop on the hook—one chain is now made.

2. Make as many chains as your pattern tells you to make. Do not count the slipknot or the loop currently on your hook as a chain. The chain is the foundation of a crocheted piece, much like the cast-on row in knitting.

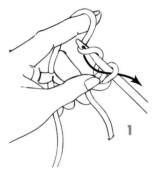

what comes next?

Learning to read your stitches

Once you learn how to count stitches (loops) on a chain and know where to insert your hook when making stitches, you are well on your way to understanding crocheting.

Counting the loops in a chain is easy if you always remember to exclude the loop on the hook and the slipknot (see illustration at left).

When it comes to inserting your hook, you already know that when you make the first chain, you work into the center of each loop. But from the first row on, you have a choice of working under both loops or under the front or back loop (see illustration below). When your pattern doesn't tell you what to do, work under both loops. You should only insert your hook under the front or back if you are directed to do so; these techniques are used to create certain decorative looks.

With this in mind, you are ready to learn the five basic crochet stitches shown below. And believe it or not, learning them is a breeze. This is because each new stitch you learn is simply one stitch higher than the previous stitch. The height of the stitch is based on how many times you wrap the yarn around the hook. Once you learn these basic stitches, you can conquer any kind of crochet stitch, because other stitches are just variations on these.

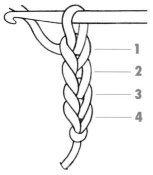

When counting chains, do not include the slipknot and the loop on the hook.

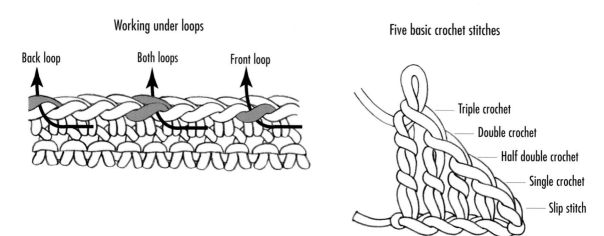

Working under loops

Back loop   Both loops   Front loop

Five basic crochet stitches

Triple crochet
Double crochet
Half double crochet
Single crochet
Slip stitch

When you complete a row of crochet stitches, you must make what's called a turning chain, abbreviated t-ch in patterns. A turning chain is a number of single chain stitches that you must make to ensure that the stitches in the next row are the same height.

Sometimes you will find the turning chain directions at the end of the directions for a row in a pattern, such as "chain 1 and turn work." ("Turn work" means exactly that: to turn the work and prepare to start another row.) In other patterns, the turning chain directions are given at the beginning of the row after you have turned the piece to begin a new row—"chain 1; work single crochet across the row." Either way, the result is the same.

The number of turning chains you need to make corresponds to the size of the stitch you are making. Here's how many turning chains you need for the basic crochet stitches:

Single crochet: one chain
Half double crochet: two chains
Double crochet: three chains
Triple crochet: four chains

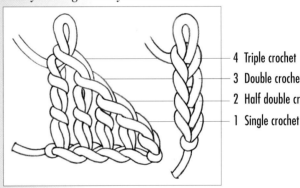

4 Triple crochet
3 Double crochet
2 Half double crochet
1 Single crochet

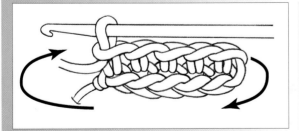

Turning the work at the end of a row of single crochet.

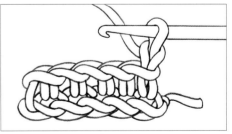

Make one chain at the beginning
or end of the row for a single crochet turning chain.

single crochet

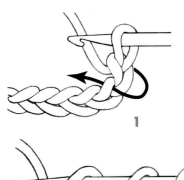

1

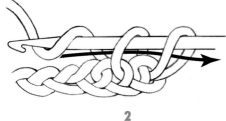

2

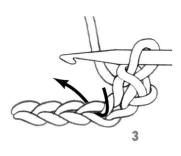

3

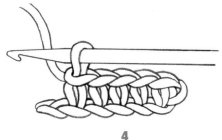

4

A versatile stitch

Single crochet is usually the first stitch you learn after making a chain. All other stitches are variations of this stitch. When worked tightly on a small hook, it can be used to make accessories such as bags and hats. If worked loosely on a larger hook, this stitch can be used to make beautiful scarves, sweaters, and throws. Let your pattern guide you in the choice of yarn and hook size.

If single crochet is required, your pattern will say, "work a single crochet in second chain from the hook."

Single crochet

1. To begin a single crochet stitch, make one more loop than is required on your foundation chain.

Holding the front side of the chain toward you (the front side looks like a loaf of braided bread; see the illustration on page 133), insert the hook into the center of the second chain (not counting the loop on the hook), from front to back.

2. Wrap the yarn once over the hook, then draw the hook through the first loop toward you. You now have two loops on the hook. Then, as shown in illustration #2, wrap the yarn the same way over the hook and draw the hook through both loops on the hook.

3. To begin the next stitch, insert the hook into the center of the next chain (do not skip one).

4. Repeat steps 1–3 until you finish the row.

To begin the second row, turn the piece around. Chain one—that is, make one plain chain stitch—before or after turning your piece to continue. Now that you have completed the first foundation row of single crochet, you will insert the hook under both loops of the row below—not into the center of the chain as before. Then just repeat steps 2–4, again not skipping any loops as you did at the start of the first foundation row.

ASK THE EXPERTS

My first piece of single crocheting is very uneven at the edges. What am I doing wrong and how can I make my next piece more even?

You are probably not working the exact number of stitches on each row. Work a single crochet stitch on top of each stitch below it. It might help you to count the stitches as you work them. In some basic stitches you make the last stitch into the turning chain, but in single crochet, you do not make a stitch into the turning chain stitch, so it's easy to lose track of the number of stitches you've done. This difference will be indicated in patterns with wording like "work into the turning chain."

The bottom edge of my first scarf is not the same width as the rest of my scarf. What happened?

As a new crocheter, it sounds like you are making your beginning chain too tightly. Try to keep the chain as loose as you can. It makes working your first row of stitches much easier. Also, count the stitches on your rows to make sure that you haven't added more stitches along the way.

I'm a left-hander and have really tried to use the right-handed method, but it's not working for me. Does this mean I should give up?

No! If you haven't been able to learn using the right-handed method, then just learn using your left. Unlike with knitting, it is actually possible to be a left-handed crocheter and work from patterns designed for right-handers. In fact, many crochet books and booklets show diagrams for both left- and right-handers. The basic difference is that instead of crocheting from right to left across a row, you will go from left to right. The hook is held in the left hand, and yarn in the right hand. You hold the hook and yarn exactly as a right-hander would, but in the opposite hand.

half double and double crochet

The next step up the ladder

Half double crochet (abbreviated as hdc) is, as you might imagine, halfway between single and double crochet. Once you have practiced single crochet, trying half double crochet is a natural next step. While this stitch is just as easy to make as single or double crochet, it is not used quite as often. You will make two turning chains at the end of the row, rather than the one you make for single crochet.

If half double crochet is required, your pattern will say, "work a half double crochet in third chain from the hook."

Half double crochet

1. To begin a half double crochet stitch, leave two loops unworked on the foundation chain. Holding the front side of the chain toward you, wrap the yarn over the hook and insert it into the center of the third chain (not counting the loop on the hook).

2. Wrap the yarn over the hook counterclockwise. Draw the yarn through the loop toward you. You now have three loops on the hook.

3. Wrap the yarn the same way over the hook. Draw the hook through all three loops on the hook—one half double crochet is now complete.

4. Insert the hook into the next chain. You will notice that the two chains you left unworked now make one stitch, so you now have two stitches done. Continue to work steps 2–4 (but do not skip chains, which you only do at the beginning of the first row) until you finish the row.

To begin the second row, turn the piece around. Chain two before or after turning your piece.

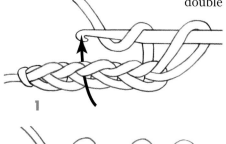

1

2

3

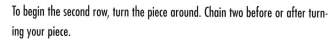

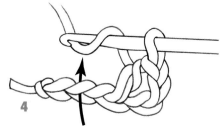

4

Double crochet (abbreviated as dc) is twice the height of single crochet. Next to single crochet, it is probably the stitch you will encounter most often. You count the turning chain as the first stitch of the row.

If double crochet is required, your pattern will say, "work a double crochet in fourth chain from the hook."

Double crochet

1. To begin a row of double crochet, leave three loops unworked on the foundation chain. Holding the front side of the chain toward you, wrap the yarn over the hook and then insert it into the center of the fourth chain (not counting the loop on the hook).

2. Wrap the yarn over the hook counterclockwise. Draw the yarn through the loop toward you. You now have three loops on the hook.

3. Wrap the yarn the same way over the hook. Draw the hook through two loops on the hook—two loops remain.

4. Put the yarn over the hook again and draw the hook through the remaining two loops—one double crochet completed.

5. Insert the hook into the next chain. You will notice that the three chains still left unworked now make one stitch, so you now have two stitches done. Continue to work steps 2–5, but do not skip chains—this is only done at the beginning of the first row.

To begin the second row, turn the piece around. Chain three before or after turning.

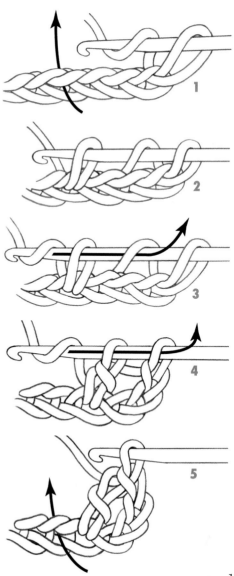

triple crochet

A higher stitch

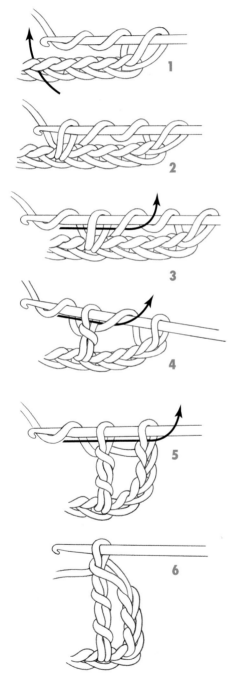

Triple crochet (abbreviated as trc) is yet a taller stitch. Another name for this stitch is "treble" crochet. A piece of fabric made in triple crochet is holier than the other stitches because of its height. You will use four turning chains at the end of the row and the turning chain counts as the first stitch.

If triple crochet is required, your pattern will say, "work a triple crochet in fifth chain from the hook."

Triple crochet

1. To begin a triple crochet, leave four loops unworked on the foundation chain. Holding the front side of the chain toward you, wrap the yarn over the hook twice counterclockwise and then insert it into the center of the fifth chain (not counting the loop on the hook).

2. Draw the yarn through the loop toward you. You now have four loops on the hook.

3. Wrap the yarn the same way over the hook. Draw the hook through two loops on the hook—three loops remain.

4. Wrap the yarn around the hook again and draw through two loops on the hook—two loops remain.

5. Wrap the yarn around the hook again and draw through two loops on the hook—one triple crochet completed.

6. You will notice that the four chains that you have left unworked make one stitch, so you now have two stitches done. Insert the hook into the next chain. Continue to work steps 2–6, but do not skip chains as you did in the first row.

To begin the second row, turn the piece around. Chain four before or after turning.

When crocheting, it's easy to add another ball of yarn or a new color. The new strand is added just before you draw the yarn through the last loops to complete a stitch. This is true for all types of stitches.

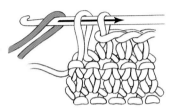

Depending on the pattern and the yarn you are using, sometimes you will need to add a new ball or color in the middle of a row, and sometimes at the end.

End of the row

When there are two loops left on the hook for the last stitch, take the new yarn and draw it through both loops. Be careful when making the turning chain that you don't pull the new yarn out. When you are done with the piece, weave in the old and new ends.

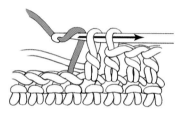

Middle of the row

While it is best to add a new strand at the beginning or end of a row, you may need to add it in the middle of the row if a pattern requires a color change. When there are two loops on the hook in the last stitch worked, add the new yarn in the same way as for the end of a row.

FIRST PERSON SUCCESS STORY

Learning Crochet Stitches

I had a hard time remembering the differences between the four basic crochet stitches, so I finally got a notebook and wrote out the differences in my own shorthand way so that I could tell them apart. I wrote: "single crochet—go into second chain from hook, draw through both loops, chain one for turning chain; double crochet—go into fourth chain from hook, yarn over and draw through two loops twice, chain three for turning chain." I referred to it over and over, and eventually it became second nature. I think the real trick is to find a shorthand or system that works for you.

—Janyce K., Staten Island, NY

slip stitch and crochet edges

Stitches with multiple uses

Crocheted edges are a nice finishing touch for pieces like throws and blankets. These stitches create a neat edge and may stabilize your piece too. They can also be used on knit pieces to create collars, cuffs, or button and buttonhole bands.

You do not have to use fancy stitches for edgings. Single crochet is often used for this purpose. Some edges are made of several rows of single crochet, with the last row worked in slip stitch or in reverse single crochet (see page 143).

Slip stitch is a versatile stitch that is good for edging; because it only minimally increases the height of your piece, it could almost be called a "nonstitch" stitch. It is also used to join circular crocheted pieces together (such as the center parts of a granny square) or to move your yarn across areas you don't want to work (for example, at an underarm indent). Because it is a flat stitch, slip stitch is also used to seam crocheted pieces together without sewing.

Slip stitch into a chain

If your pattern calls for slip stitch on an unworked chain, insert the hook through the center of the last stitch in the chain. Wrap the yarn over the hook and pull the yarn through the chain and the loop on the hook in one motion. Repeat this step for the second slip stitch and for as many as you need to make.

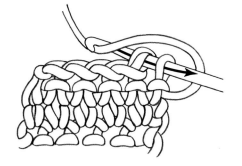

Slip stitch into a stitch

If your pattern calls for slip stitch into a row of, say, single crochet or another stitch, insert the hook under both loops of the stitch. Wrap the yarn over the hook and pull the yarn through the stitch and the loop on the hook in one motion. Repeat this step as many times as required.

REVERSE SINGLE CROCHET

Sometimes a pattern will call for reverse single crochet, or crab stitch, which is basically backward single crochet—meaning that instead of working right to left, you work left to right. This will give your edge a slightly bumpier, firmer look. Here's how to do it:

1. If you're starting this stitch at the end of a row, chain one and do not turn the piece. (This means you will be working the following steps from left to right.) Insert the hook into the last stitch you made.

2. Wrap the yarn once over the hook and pull through a loop.

3. Yarn over the hook again, and draw the yarn through both loops. One loop remains.

4. Insert the hook into the next stitch and yarn over the hook.

5. Continue in this way along the piece until you have finished the edge.

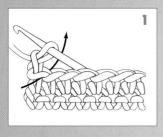
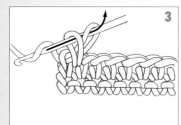

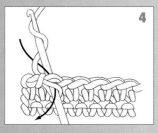
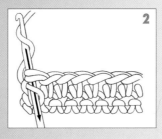
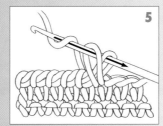

CHAIN AND EDGING TIPS

- Use chains for ties, straps, and drawstrings.
- To make extra-thick chains, hold several strands of yarn together.
- Make a chain and then slip stitch into the chain to make a hat tie, cord, etc.
- Attach pom-poms or tassels to the ends of chains for hat straps.
- Braid several different colored chains together to make a bag strap.
- Try to space your edge stitches evenly as you work. If they look floppy or tight, unravel them and try again.
- Use edgings to cover uneven side stitches and keep scarves from rolling.
- Try an edge made of several rows of single crochet, each row in a different color.
- Work two or three edge stitches in a corner, one stitch next to another in the same stitch, to create a neatly rounded edge.

fastening off and seaming

Wrapping it up

If you're crocheting a flat piece, such as a scarf, throw, or blanket, finishing it off is easy—you just have to fasten off the last stitch. When you finish the last stitch, cut the yarn (leaving a few inches to weave into the piece) and pull it through the last loop. Weave the yarn into the side seam just as you would do when knitting (see page 65).

Flat pieces don't usually require sewing unless they are made out of individual patches that must be joined together. But if you do need to sew, you have several options. First, review the preparation techniques on pages 100–101 to get your piece or pieces ready to sew. You can use the same techniques you would use for preparing to sew knitted pieces.

How you sew crocheted pieces together depends on the type of seam you want to make. For example, if you are joining squares for a blanket, you might use a crochet hook to join them using slip stitch or single crochet. This is a fast way to join squares and creates a decorative look on a throw or blanket, in which both sides show. For a sweater, sewing with a needle is a better choice, because it creates a seam that is less bulky. Whatever you decide, try to get your seam as flat and even as possible.

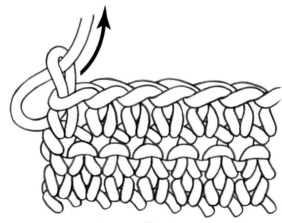

Fastening off the last stitch

SEAMING TECHNIQUES

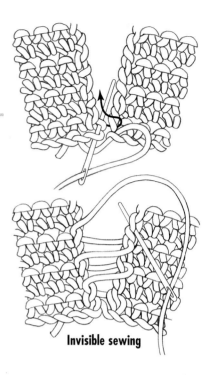

Invisible sewing with a needle

1. Line up the two pieces to be joined side-by-side, with the right sides facing you.
2. Thread a large-eyed blunt needle. Attach the yarn to one edge by running the yarn in and out of the edge where you want to begin. Do not make a knot.
3. Insert the needle through the lowest edge stitch on the opposite piece.
4. Insert the needle through the next edge stitch on the first piece.
5. Continue up the seam, going from side to side in a zigzag pattern, catching the edge stitch each time. (However, if your edge is very uneven, you may want to seam one stitch in from the edge.)

Invisible sewing

Slip stitch seam

1. Line up the two pieces to be joined side-by-side, wrong sides facing out.
2. Insert your hook through the edge stitches of both pieces. Wrap the yarn over the hook and draw through a loop.
3. Insert the hook into the next edge stitch of both pieces. Wrap the yarn over the hook and draw it through both the fabrics and the loop on the hook.
4. Continue along the piece until the seam is complete.

Slip stitch

Single crochet at the edges

1. Line up the two pieces to be joined side-by-side, wrong sides facing out.
2. Insert your hook through the fabric of both pieces. Wrap the yarn over the hook and draw through a loop.
3. Insert the hook into the next edge stitch of both pieces. Wrap the yarn over the hook and pull up a loop of yarn.
4. Wrap the yarn over the hook and draw it through the loops on the hook—one single crochet is complete.
5. Continue along the piece until the seam is complete. This will make a somewhat thicker seam.

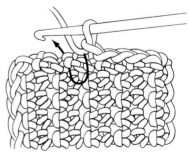

Single crochet

adding and subtracting stitches

Increasing and decreasing in crochet

By adding or subtracting the number of stitches in a row, you can change the shape of your crochet piece. It is really simple to do. The examples shown here are in single crochet, but the technique is the same for any basic stitch. This type of increasing or decreasing is generally done within a piece, as opposed to on an edge. Your pattern will usually tell you where to increase or decrease in a row.

Increasing one stitch in single crochet

1. Make the first single crochet as you would normally make it (see page 136), then insert the hook into the same stitch again.

2. Wrap the yarn over the hook and pull up a loop. Wrap the yarn again draw it through both loops on the hook.

3. You now have made two stitches in the same stitch, which means you've added one stitch. On the next row, make single crochets above both stitches.

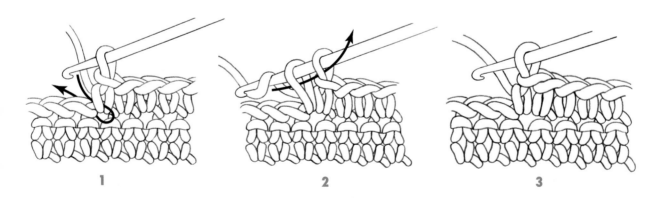

1   2   3

Decreasing one stitch in single crochet

1. Insert the hook into the first stitch. Wrap the yarn over the hook and pull up a loop. Repeat the process in the next stitch. You now have three loops on the hook.

2. Place the yarn over the hook and draw it through all three loops.

3. You now have one stitch less. On the next row, you will make only one single crochet above the new stitch.

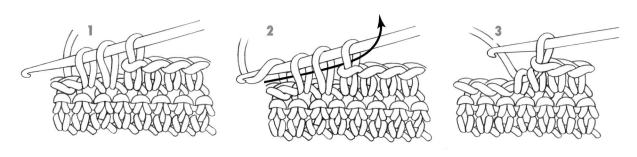

COUNTING ROWS AND STITCHES

To take the gauge on a crochet swatch (see pages 66–67), you need to be able to identify the stitches and rows. Luckily, rows and stitches are usually very well defined on a crochet piece and easy to see. Higher stitches, such as double and triple crochet, actually have a little space between each stitch that makes it even easier to count.

However, if you are using a yarn that does not show the stitches well, such as a highly textured yarn, you might want to count the rows as you make them. You can keep track of them on a piece of paper as you crochet. When working with a textured yarn, you can take the measurement for the gauge swatch over the entire piece widthwise and lengthwise instead of counting specific stitches and rows.

12 rows in single crochet (top right)
6 rows in double crochet (bottom right)

popcorns, bobbles, and clusters

Texture stitches in crochet

Textured stitches are easy to crochet. They make great allover fabric, or accents when used in combination with basic stitches. The common denominator here is that they are all made of several stitches joined together to give them a puffy look. There are two basic ways to make them. You can either make each stitch inside the same stitch, over and over, or make a number of separate stitches, then join them at the top. This first way creates more dimension, and is the most common way to make these textured stitches.

Although the examples given here are all done in double crochet, you can make them using half double or triple crochet too.

Popcorn

A popcorn is a series of stitches worked inside the same stitch, which creates a popcornlike appearance.

1. Make five double crochets inside one stitch.

2. Take the hook out of the loop on the last double crochet. Insert the hook (from front to back) under the top loop of the first double crochet and back into the loop on the hook. Wrap the yarn over the hook and draw it through the loop on the hook and through the first double crochet. This anchors the popcorn and gives it a dimensional appearance.

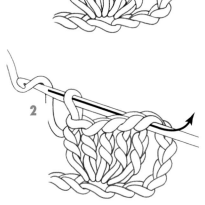

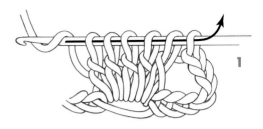

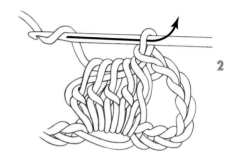

Bobble

Similar to a popcorn stitch, a bobble is made by working a series of stitches inside one stitch, then joining them at the end.

1. Make five double crochets inside one stitch, but instead of completing each stitch, leave one loop of each stitch on the hook. Once the five double crochets are completed, wrap the yarn over the hook and draw it through all six loops on the hook.

2. Place the yarn over the hook and draw it through the remaining loop—a chain one is made. Continue on with your pattern.

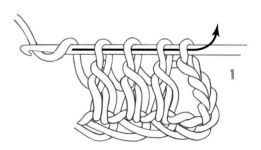

Cluster Stitch

The cluster stitch is made of individual stitches, rather than several stitches in one stitch. The stitches are partially made and then joined at the end.

1. Make three double crochets in each of the next three stitches, leaving the last loop in each series on the hook. You now have four loops on the hook. Wrap the yarn over the hook and draw it through all the loops.

2. You do not need to make a chain one, just continue with the next stitch in your pattern.

my first crochet scarf

A great two-toned look

Size

5" x 72" (without fringe)

Materials

- 1 ball of Lion Brand Wool-Ease Chunky
  86% Acrylic, 10% Wool, 4% Rayon
  5 oz (140 g) – 153 yds (140 m)
  #402 Wheat
- 1 ball of Lion Brand Wool-Ease Chunky
  80% Acrylic, 20% Wool
  5 oz (140 g) – 153 yds (140 m)
  #107 Bluebell
- Size P-15 (10 mm) crochet hook,
  or size to get gauge

Gauge

8 stitches and 6 rows = 4" (10 cm) in half double crochet (but don't worry too much about gauge for this one, as scarf sizes don't have to be exact)

Notes

1. Before you begin, cut 24 strands of each color yarn by wrapping the yarn lengthwise around a video box.
2. When you have finished making your scarf, instead of weaving in the beginning and the ending yarn tails, just add them to the fringe.

Scarf

Using the Wheat yarn, make a slipknot and chain 12.

First Row Work a half double crochet in the third chain from the hook and in the next 9 chains—10 half double crochets completed. Chain 2, turn the piece.

(Note: The chain 2 counts as the first half double crochet stitch of the next row.)

Row 2 Working into the half double crochets of the previous row, make 9 half double crochet stitches—a total of 10 half double crochets. Chain 2, turn the piece.

Repeat row 2 until the scarf measures 36". End the last row before making the chain 2. Cut the yarn and tie on the Bluebell color.

With Bluebell, chain 2 and turn the piece. Continue working row 2 in Bluebell until the scarf measures 72". Fasten off the last stitch.

Fringe

Make 6 fringes along each end of the scarf, using 2 strands of each color yarn for each fringe (see page 105 on fringe).

now what do I do?

Answers to common questions

As a beginner, what should I consider when choosing projects?

First, pick a project that will not take too long to complete. Accessories make great beginner projects. Use a yarn without a lot of texture so you can easily see the stitches. Check the skill rating and choose beginner or easy projects. If the pattern does not indicate a level, review it before beginning. Stay away from projects that have lengthy patterns or a great deal of shaping. Your first crocheting attempts should be easy, fun, and quick.

My friends tell me that crocheting is faster than knitting. Is this true?

There are some very fast knitters, as well as crocheters, but crocheting might qualify as a slightly faster craft. Working with just one hook rather than two needles does give you somewhat of an advantage. Also, by making taller stitches, you certainly are able to crochet a longer piece faster than you can knit one. Knit rows only grow in height in proportion to the needle size and yarn thickness.

What's the easiest type of crochet hook to learn with—wood, plastic, or metal?

None of these is especially easier to work with than the others. You might try out a couple different ones to see which you prefer. Certain yarns are a little slippery (like rayon and silk blends), so you may find a plastic or wood hook easier to maneuver. Some hooks have special shafts for easier holding by those with hand problems or arthritis. These types of hooks are also nice if you are a beginner.

What are some good ways to combine basic crochet with my knitting projects?

Even if you never make a crocheted project, learning to crochet is very helpful for knitters. You can make edges, straps, borders, cuffs, and collars with crochet stitches. Crocheting along an edge is a great way to stabilize a knit piece. Plus, you can make attractive button and buttonhole bands on a cardigan, or attach knit pieces together using crocheted seams. The two crafts work very well together.

NOW WHERE DO I GO?

WEB SITES

www.crochet.about.com

www.woolery.com/booksknit.html
Offers a range of books on learning to crochet.

BOOKS

Crochet Your Way
By Gloria Tracy and Susan Levin
This crochet bible will get you off to a good start.
It has a great stitch sampler project that you can
use to make a unique throw.

How to Crochet
By Pauline Turner
This book gives you good basics and easy projects
as you move through each of the 10 workshops.

*The Harmony Guide to 300
Crochet Stitches*
By the staff of Collins and Brown Ltd.
This beginner's paperback has lots of stitches,
photos, and basic techniques.

*The Harmony Guide to 220 More
Crochet Stitches*
By the staff of Collins and Brown Ltd.
The second in the series. All Harmony guides are
good additions to your needlecraft library.

Chapter 9
CROCHETED GRANNY SQUARES

a versatile motif

They're not just for grannies

Granny squares were probably invented by thrifty needlecrafters who wanted to use their leftover bits of yarn. Eventually, they realized they could make beautiful afghans simply by crocheting those bits into squares—in much the same way that quilters use small pieces of extra fabric to make quilts.

Granny squares have been around for ages. They were especially fashionable in the '70s, when they were used to make everything from afghans to vests. Even though these colorful creations went into hiding for a time, they never completely disappeared, and they're making a big comeback these days. They're now used to make fun accessories, home decor items, and even sweaters. Other trendy granny square items include skirts, bags, and ponchos.

One reason granny squares continue to be popular is that they are a cinch to make, even if you do not have much crocheting experience. In fact, once you learn the basic steps, making a granny square blanket or bag as your first real project is not a bad idea.

The yarns used to make granny squares vary as much as the techniques used to create them. Thinner yarns are good for smaller squares, while thicker yarns make chunkier ones. You can stitch them up quickly, especially if you use larger hooks and a heavier weight yarn. The kind of yarn you should choose also depends on your project—for example, use washable acrylic yarn for a throw, and cotton for a hat or bag.

A quick warning: One disadvantage to using granny squares is that you have to join them together, which does take time. When making a large project such as a throw, it is sometimes easier to join them in stages, rather than waiting until you've made all the squares.

■ "Granny square" is a bit of a misnomer; in this motif, the first row is actually a circle

■ On each additional row (or round) after the center circle, four corners are added to turn it into a square.

■ You don't turn the work around after working each row—you just continue to crochet in the same direction.

■ Increases are made in every row.

■ The right side of a square will always be facing you as you make it—you never work with the back side facing you.

■ You can change colors as often as you want. You can work every round in a new color, change colors every few rows, or use the same color throughout.

■ Traditional granny square throws are made up of squares that have colorful centers, with the last round worked in black.

■ Granny squares sometimes have a flowerlike appearance when worked with a central bright color and outer "leaf" rounds in green.

■ They can be made in a wide range of sizes—as small as an inch or two across, or as wide as a yard or more.

■ Be creative! Incorporate different size squares in the same project.

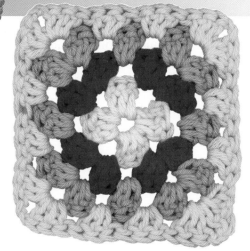

granny square basics

Reviewing what you know already

You do not need to know many crochet techniques or any special stitches to make granny squares, just the basics. Before you begin, review the following:

- Making a slipknot (see page 133)
- Working a chain (see page 133)
- Slip stitch (see page 142)
- Double crochet (see page 139)
- Single crochet (if you want to add a decorative edge, see page 142)
- Seaming with a needle or crochet hook (see page 145)

The center of a granny square is made of crochet chains. The number of chains varies, but it's most often four to six. The more chains you use, the larger the center hole. If you use too few stitches, it will be difficult to work the first row of stitches in the small circle you've made.

Also remember not to make the chain too tight, because you need to be able to join the chain to make a ring. When counting the chains, omit the slipknot and the last chain on the hook.

When making a granny square, use double crochet stitches throughout, and slip stitches to join a new row to the row you've just finished.

MAKING THE CENTER RING

1. Make a slipknot and then make the number of chains you need (in this illustration, there are six chains).

2. Leaving the chain on the hook, insert the hook through the first chain (the one just above the slipknot). Place the yarn over the hook. Draw the hook through both loops. This is the joining slip stitch. This closes the circle so that you are ready to begin the first row.

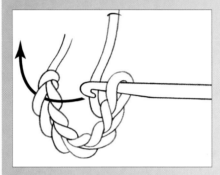 

IS IT A ROW OR A ROUND?

In standard crocheting, you make rows of stitches. When you crochet a granny square or any other circular pattern, you are also making rows. However, because the rows are made in a circular fashion without turning the piece around to begin a new row, each row is a called a round, often abbreviated "rnd" in patterns. A slip stitch joins the last stitch in the round to the first stitch, creating a circle.

moving out

Going beyond the inner circle

The first round of a granny square beyond the center ring is also a circle, but the way you make it paves the way for turning the circle into a square. And the steps for this round prepare you to work all the remaining rows in the square.

Making the first round

1. Once you have joined the center circle, make three chains. These three chains will become your first double crochet stitch.

2. Wrap the yarn over the hook as you would for a double crochet stitch. Hold the circle in your left hand. Insert the hook through the center of the circle, wrap the yarn, and pull up a loop. There will be three loops on the hook.

3. Yarn over* and draw it through two loops. You will now have two loops on the hook.

4. Yarn over and draw through two loops again—one loop remains and one double crochet is completed.

5. Make another double crochet into the circle, repeating steps 2–4. Three double crochets are now completed (including one made from the first three chains).

6. Make two chains. This creates a space between the next group of three double crochets that you will make.

7. Repeat steps 2–6 twice more. This means that will have four groups of three double crochets going around the circle. If it seems like you don't have enough space to make the last set of double crochets, gently push the stitches around the circle to make more room.

8. Finish by making two more chains and working a slip stitch into the third stitch in the chain three that you worked in the beginning.

9. Cut the yarn and fasten off (see page 144). Your first round is complete!

* "Yarn over" is crochet lingo for "wrap the yarn over the hook."

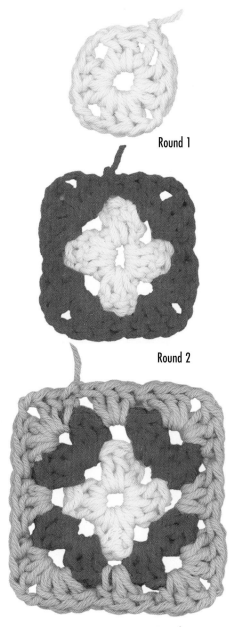

Round 1

Round 2

Round 3

Each round after the first round is made in more or less the same way. You will always have four corners, but with each round, you will add another set of side stitches between the corners. This is how your square continues to get larger while remaining flat and square. Here's how you do it:

1. Using a new color of yarn, put your hook under the chain-two space made in step 6 of the first round and pull up a loop of the new color, leaving a tail of a few inches.

2. Chain three. As you did in the first round, work two double crochets into the same chain-two space.

3. Chain two and then work three double crochets in this same chain-two space—the first corner is complete.

4. To make the next corner, work three double crochets in the next chain-two space, chain two, then work another set of three double crochets in the same space.

5. Repeat step 4 twice more to make the last two corners. Use a slip stitch to join the last double crochet to the top of the first chain three.

6. Cut the yarn and fasten off.

ROUND THREE AND BEYOND

When it's time to add the third round, the only difference is that in addition to the four corners, you will need to work an extra group of three double crochets in the space between each corner. Then, with each additional round after that, you will add yet another group of three double crochets. As the square gets bigger, you will have more room on each side to add these extra groups of stitches.

beyond the basic square

Variations on a theme

Once you've learned how to make a basic granny square, it opens the door to learning hundreds of variations—from squares with three-dimensional flowers in the center to ones with bold geometrical patterns.

You can also use your creativity to turn your squares into unique projects. For example, by taking the basic granny square and changing the size or the number of squares used, you can create some interesting effects. Take a look at the throw on page 170: This is actually made of one large square with a giant hook and a few strands of yarn held together.

When making a granny square project, all the squares don't necessarily have to be the same size. For example, you can make larger squares and groups of smaller ones that, when joined together in groups of four, are the same size as the larger square. Just remember that if you are making a square or rectangular piece, the sizes of the different squares will need to work together in order to maintain the shape.

Also keep in mind that you do not have to use granny squares by themselves in a project. For instance, you can join squares with several rows of stitches. And a border of granny squares is a great way to begin a knit or crocheted sweater or wrap.

ASK THE EXPERTS

I love making granny squares, but I hate having to weave in the ends that are created by cutting the yarn after every row. Any tips?

It's true, working in all the ends is not much fun. One way to cut down on this is to cover them up with stitches as you work. To do this, lay the end on top of the last round you worked. As you go into each space and work your groups of three double crochets, cover the tail end with your stitches. It's best if the tail is long enough to be worked into two groups of stitches. Snip any remaining yarn. When you have finished the square, you'll find that most of the finishing has already been done.

I have been looking for some new granny square patterns to try, and I noticed that some of them call for different numbers of corner chains. Some even have chains between side stitches. Is this okay?

Yes, just follow the instructions and you should be fine. Creating more chains will result in a lacier, more open square, and using fewer chains results in a slightly more compact square. Of course, this also depends on the yarn used. A granny square made with thicker yarn and three chains in a corner will be less open than one made of a finer-weight yarn with the same number of chains.

I have a hard time identifying the beginning three chains in each round, so I'm never exactly sure where I'm supposed to make the slip stitch to finish the round. Help!

Placing a small safety pin in the first chain 3 should help. Move it up with each new round that you do. After a while, it will be easier to spot the three chains, and then you can stop using the pin. Until this becomes easier for you, use smooth, untextured yarns so that you can clearly see all the stitches and changes.

joining squares

When your squares are done, the next step is to join them together in some fashion. You can either stitch them together with a needle, or crochet them together using matching yarn (see crochet seaming techniques on pages 144–145).

How you join your squares is somewhat a matter of taste and also depends on the finished look you are trying to achieve. If you have many squares to join and you want to do it quickly, crocheting them together is the most practical choice. Sewing with a needle is better when you want both sides to look neat, such as when you are making a scarf.

If your squares look uneven, you can work an edge around them to make them more uniform. Usually this type of edge is made in single crochet (learn more about crocheted edges on pages 142–143).

When making a piece such as a throw, where there are many squares to join together, sew a row of squares at a time, set it aside, then sew the next row. Then sew the two rows together. Continue in this way until you have them all joined.

In places where four squares meet, take care to even out the corners and smooth out any lumpiness so that the edges match up neatly.

In many patterns, you will need to create a number of squares—sometimes 10 or more—in the same color sequence. It's easier to keep track of them if they are piled flat. Use plastic zipper bags to separate them by color or type. Label each bag with an identifying number (sometimes the pattern will provide a number for each type of square). Then store the bags neatly in a box or container to keep them flat and clean. Organizing them this way helps a lot when it's time to assemble your project.

FIRST PERSON SUCCESS STORY

The Legacy Lives On

My mother started making an afghan for me when I was a teenager. Twenty years later, it still wasn't finished! So when she found out that I had learned to crochet, she brought it over in pieces with the remaining yarn. Luckily, she still had the pattern. I had a great time completing the project, which now adorns my bedside chair, and love the fact that both my mother and I worked it. I plan to use this same pattern to start an afghan for my own 10-year-old daughter to finish someday.

—**Carrie P., Sacramento, CA**

a granny square scarf

Simple squares make an eye-catching scarf

Size
4" x 75"

Materials
- 1 ball each of Mission Falls/Unique Kolours
1824 Wool
  100% Merino Superwash Wool
  $1^3/_4$ oz (50 g) – 85 yds (78 m)
  #003 Taupe (A)
  #016 Light Olive (B)
   #020 Light Teal (C)
    #021 Teal (D)
    #012 Brick (E)
    #024 Eggplant (F)
- Size H-8 (5 mm) crochet hook,
  or size to get gauge
- Large-eyed, blunt needle (for sewing squares)

Gauge
1 square = 4" (10 cm)

Square sequences
Make 3 squares in each color sequence.

Square	Round 1	Round 2	Round 3	Round 4
#1	A	F	C	D
#2	B	D	A	E
#3	E	B	F	C
#4	D	B	E	F
#5	F	C	D	B
#6	C	E	B	A

Notes

Work each round in the color noted in the chart. Note that the pattern for the granny square used here is slightly different than the basic one on page 160.

Squares

Chain 5.

Round 1 Join chain into a ring with a slip stitch; chain 3, work 2 double crochet; work the following 3 times—chain 1, work 3 double crochet; end chain 1 and join to top of chain 3 with a slip stitch. Fasten off the yarn.

Round 2 With second color and beginning in next chain 1 space, chain 3, work 2 double crochet in chain 1 space, chain 2, work 3 double crochet in the same chain 1 space; in the next 3 corners work as follows—work 3 double crochet, chain 2, work 3 double crochet; join to top of chain 3 with a slip stitch. Fasten off the yarn.

Round 3 With third color and beginning in next chain 1 space, chain 3, work 2 double crochet in chain 1 space, chain 2, work 3 double crochet in the same chain 1 space; work the following 3 times—work 3 double crochet in next space, then [work 3 double crochet, chain 2, work 3 double crochet] in the corner over the chain 2 space; work 3 double crochet in last space; join to top of chain 3 with a slip stitch. Fasten off the yarn.

Round 4 With fourth color and beginning in next chain 1 space, chain 3, work 2 double crochet in chain 1 space, chain 2, work 3 double crochet in the same chain 1 space; work the following 3 times—work 3 double crochet in next 3 spaces, then [work 3 double crochet, chain 2, work 3 double crochet] in the corner over the chain 2 space; work 3 double crochet in last two spaces; join to top of chain 3 with a slip stitch. Fasten off the yarn. Set square aside.

Finishing

Weave in ends.

Sew squares 1–6 together, then repeat sequence twice.

With color D, work 1 row of single crochet around entire scarf, beginning halfway along the edge of the first square. Work 3 single crochets in each corner to make a square corner. Fasten off and work in remaining ends.

Fringe

Cut several strands of the various colors of yarn by wrapping the yarn lengthwise around a video box and cutting along one end. Make fringes along the short ends of the scarf, using 4 different colored strands of yarn for each fringe (see page 105 on fringe).

a road map for squares

Simplifying things with charts

Many granny square patterns, particularly newer ones, have not only written instructions, but visual charts like the one shown here—a boon for those who learn best via diagrams or illustrations.

This chart contains the same instructions as those on page 160 for the basic granny square. A chart like this is a visual representation of the stitches that make up the granny square. Here, it shows that each granny square will have four rounds, plus a center ring.

The key next to the chart tells you what the symbols in each round mean, and whether you need to make a double crochet, slip stitch, or chain.

To get a sense of how to work with charts like this, read each round from where it begins around to the left, until you are back at the beginning again. After you have worked from a few charts like this, you may find it easier than working from written instructions.

GRANNY SQUARE PATTERN

○ Chain

⊤ Double crochet

● Slip stitch

JUST A FEW THINGS YOU CAN MAKE WITH GRANNY SQUARES

- scarves
- bags
- coin and key purses
- book and box covers
- placemats
- coasters
- table runners and tablecloths
- pillow and cushion covers
- hats
- headbands
- wrist and neck warmers
- shawls and wraps
- ponchos
- skirts
- rugs
- blankets and throws

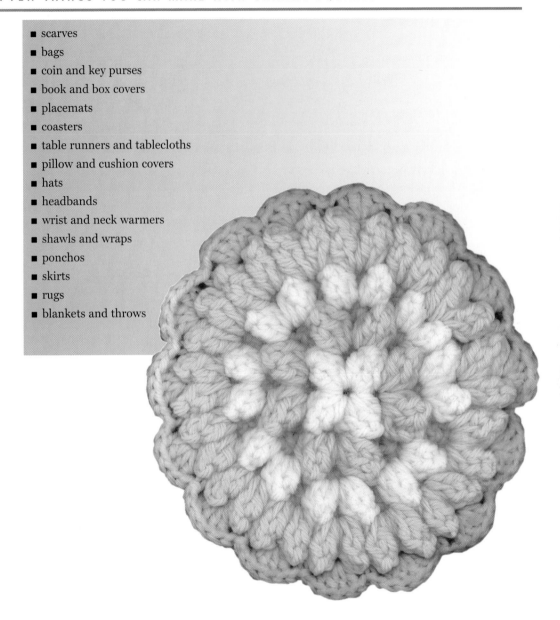

a giant granny throw
Quick crocheting with a large hook

Size
54" x 54"

Materials
- Lion Brand Homespun
  98% Acrylic, 2% Polyester
  6 oz (170 g) – 185 yds (167 m)
  2 skeins of #363 Sandstone
  4 skeins of #318 Sierra
  4 skeins of #312 Edwardian
- Size Q-19 (15 mm) crochet hook,
  or size to get gauge
- Large-eyed, blunt needle
  (for weaving in ends)

Gauge
3 double crochet = 4" (10 cm)
using 2 strands of Homespun

Notes
1. Hold 2 strands of yarn and work with them held together throughout.

2. Repeat instructions in [ ] as many times as indicated following the brackets.

3. Work 9 rounds in Sandstone, 6 rounds in Sierra, and 4 rounds in Edwardian.

4. Work the edging in Edwardian.

Throw

With 2 strands of yarn held together, chain 4. Slip stitch in the 4th chain from the hook to make a ring.

Round 1 Chain 3 (this counts as the first double crochet), work 2 double crochet in the ring, chain 1, [work 3 double crochet, chain 1] 3 times. Slip stitch in the top of the chain 3. Slip stitch in the next 2 double crochet and then slip stitch into the chain-1 space.

Round 2 Working into the chain-1 space, chain 3, work 2 double crochet in the ring, chain 1, work 3 double crochet; [chain 1, 3 double crochet, chain 1, 3 double crochet] in each of the next 3 corner spaces, end chain 1. Slip stitch in the top of the chain 3. Slip stitch in the next 2 double crochet and then slip stitch into the chain-1 space.

Round 3 Working into the chain-1 space, chain 3, work 2 double crochet in the ring, chain 1, work 3 double crochet; *[chain 1, 3 double crochet, chain 1] in next chain 1 space, [3 double crochet, chain 1, 3 double crochet] in next corner space; repeat from the * twice, ending [chain 1, 3 double crochet, chain 1] in next chain-1 space. Slip stitch in the next 2 double crochet and into the chain-1 space.

Continue to work in one big square, repeating round 3, adding 1 additional [chain 1, 3 double crochet, chain 1] in next chain-1 space each round.

Border

Round 1 Working with 2 strands of yarn, chain 1 [1 single crochet, chain 1, 2 single crochet] in first chain-1 corner, [single crochet in each double crochet and chain-1 space to next corner, (2 single crochet, chain 1, 2 single crochet) in corner chain-1 space] 3 times. Continue single crochet to end of round, slip stitch to first chain 1. Slip stitch to corner chain, chain 1.

Round 2 Work as round 1. Slip stitch to first chain 1 to join. Fasten off. Weave in ends.

now what do I do?

Answers to common questions

My granny square throw pattern includes a chart in which each square has a different number. How can I use this to assemble the pieces easily when I have finished all the squares?

A chart such as the one you describe is a valuable road map for making and joining your squares. Try this handy trick: Make a copy of the chart and color-code the squares. For instance, if all the #1 squares have yellow centers, shade those squares in yellow on your chart. Then, when you're ready to assemble your throw, all you need to do is refer to the colors on your chart, instead of trying to assemble it by number.

Not all my finished squares are the same size, even though I used the same number of stitches and rows. What did I do wrong?

You probably didn't do anything wrong—you probably just changed your tension a bit while working on different squares. This tends to happen when you work squares at different times; say, with a few weeks or months in between. If the difference is not too great, don't be too concerned. Just try to even them out as you sew them together by stretching the shorter edge slightly. Or, if the squares are made of wool, dampen them and then shape them slightly to make them all the same size. If one or two squares are a lot bigger or smaller than the rest, make new squares to replace them.

Can I use yarns in variegated colors to make granny squares?

Yes, this is a great way to create a multicolor look without having to change colors frequently. Variegated yarns look best when teamed with at least one solid color. For example, you might choose a colorful variegated yarn for the center, then make all the last rows in a solid color such as black or navy. The look will be dramatic. Before you embark on a complete project, consider getting one ball of each of the variegated and solid shades and making some sample squares. When worked, and when placed next to a solid color, the variegated shades may look very different.

Can I make granny squares using just one color? If so, do I need to use a different technique?

Yes, you can make one-color granny squares, and the only big difference is that you do not have to cut the yarn after each round. After joining the round, work several slip stitches into the next space and make three chains to begin the round. This is a very easy way to make granny squares. Just keep in mind that the squares will have a much different look. One interesting effect is to work one-color squares and multicolor squares and combine them in the same project.

NOW WHERE DO I GO?

WEB SITES

www.crochetcabana.com
Scroll down and click on "The Granny Square" to view step-by-step photos for making a granny square.

www.allcrafts.net/crochetknit.htm
Scroll down and click on "Classic Crochet Granny Squares."

BOOKS

Adorable Crochet for Babies and Toddlers
By Lesley Stanfield
This book has nice simple crochet projects including an easy granny square blanket and baby blocks.

The Complete Idiot's Guide to Knitting and Crocheting (Second Edition)
By Barbara Breiter and Gail Diven
A volume with lots of "nuts and bolts" info, and helpful tips on making motifs such as granny squares.

Crocheting in Plain English
By Maggie Righetti
Full of good sound advice and includes illustrations and info on making granny squares.

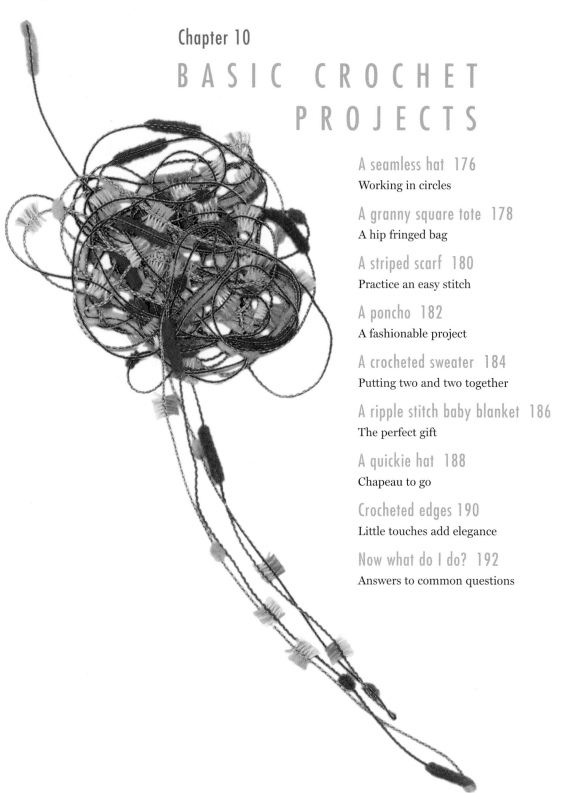

Chapter 10

BASIC CROCHET
PROJECTS

a seamless hat

No seam needed here

Size

S/M (L)

Materials

- 1 ball of Lion Brand Wool-Ease
  Thick & Quick
  20% Wool, 80% Acrylic
  6 oz (170 g) – 108 yds (98 m)
  #145 Plum
- Size P-15 (10 mm) crochet hook,
  or size to get gauge
- Large-eyed, blunt needle (for sewing)

Gauge

8 single crochet = 4" (10 cm)

Notes

This hat is worked as a spiral. Use a safety pin to identify the end of the round. Move the pin each time you come to the end of a new round.

Hat

Chain 4 and join with a slip stitch to form ring, being careful not to twist the chain.

Round 1 Work 6 single crochet into the ring.

Round 2 Work 2 single crochet in each single crochet around—12 single crochet.

Round 3 [Work 1 single crochet in next single crochet, work 2 single crochet in next single crochet] 6 times—18 single crochet.

Round 4 [Work 1 single crochet in next 2 single crochet, work 2 single crochet in next single crochet] 6 times—24 single crochet.

Round 5 [Work 1 single crochet in next 3 single crochet, work 2 single crochet in next single crochet] 6 times—30 single crochet.

Round 6 [Work 1 single crochet in next 4 single crochet, work 2 single crochet in next single crochet] 6 times—36 single crochet.

Note

For size S/M, work even on 36 single crochet until hat measures 8" from top of ring.

Round 7 (size Large only) [Work 1 single crochet in next 5 single crochet, work 2 single crochet in next single crochet] 6 times—42 single crochet.

Note

For size L, work even on 42 single crochet until hat measures 9" from top of ring.

Brim

Next round (turning point for brim) Work a single crochet in each single crochet around, working in front loop of stitch only.

Next round Work a single crochet in each single crochet around, working in both loops of stitch.

Next round [Work 1 single crochet in next 5 (6) single crochet, work 2 single crochet in next single crochet] 6 times—42 (48) single crochet.

Next round Work a single crochet in each single crochet around, joining last single crochet to beginning of round with a slip stitch. Chain 1.

Last round Work a single crochet in each single crochet around, joining last single crochet to beginning of round with a slip stitch.

Fasten off. Weave in ends.

a granny square tote

Squares with a twist

Size

10 1/2" x 10 1/2" without fringe and strap

Materials

■ 1 ball each of Lion Brand Lion Cotton 100%
5 oz (140 g) – 236 yds (212 m)

#098 Natural (A)

#158 Banana (B)

#153 Black (C)

#112 Poppy Red (D)

■ Size G-6 (4.5 mm) crochet hook,
or size to get gauge

■ One 1" or larger black button

■ Large-eyed, blunt needle (for sewing)

Gauge

Each motif (granny square) measures 3 1/2"
across

Granny Squares

Make 6 of each color combination (18 total).

Motif	#1	#2	#3
Round 1	A	B	D
Round 2	C	A	B
Round 3	B	C	A
Round 4	D	D	D

Notes

When working rounds 2 and 3, you may want to break down the steps into smaller segments. For example, do this when you are required to repeat a string of instructions in brackets a certain number of times by writing down each section on index cards that you flip over as you complete each segment. After you have made one or two squares, it gets a lot easier.

Granny Square Tote

Chain 5, join with a slip stitch in fifth chain from hook to form ring.

Round 1 Chain 1, work 8 single crochet into ring. Join with a slip stitch in first single crochet. Fasten off.

Round 2 Join next color with a slip stitch in any single crochet, chain 6, double crochet in same single crochet, [(double crochet, chain 1, double crochet) in next single crochet, (double crochet, chain 3, double crochet) in next single crochet], repeat the instructions in [ ] twice more, (double crochet, chain 1, double crochet) in next single crochet. Join with slip stitch in third chain of the beginning chain 6. Fasten off.

Round 3 Join next color with slip stitch in any chain-3 space, (chain 3, 2 double crochet, chain 3, 3 double crochet) in same space, chain 1, 3 double crochet in next chain 1 space, chain 1, [(3 double crochet, chain 3, 3 double crochet) in next chain-3 space, chain 1, 3 double crochet in next chain-1 space, chain 1] repeat the instructions in [ ] twice more, join with a slip stitch to top of the beginning chain 3. Fasten off.

Round 4 Join color D with a slip stitch in any chain-3 space, chain 1, 3 single crochet in each chain-3 space and 1 single crochet in each double crochet and chain-1 space around. Join with a slip stitch to top of the beginning single crochet. Fasten off.

Assembly

Sew motifs together into 2 large squares of 9 squares each, following chart below. From the wrong side, sew squares together along 3 sides, and then turn right side out.

Joining chart

1	3	2
3	2	1
2	1	3

Trim and strap

With color D, beginning in either corner, work 1 row single crochet around tote opening, join last single crochet to first single crochet with slip stitch.

Do not fasten off, chain 120, join strap to opposite side with slip stitch in corner, 2 single crochet, single crochet in each chain back across strap, slip stitch into chain next to first slip stitch. Turn piece and work another row of single crochet along strap, slip stitch into side. Fasten off.

Button loop

Holding 2 strands of color D together, chain 10. Fasten off.

Sew both ends of the loop to top center of center square.

Sew button to top center of center square on opposite side of bag.

Fringe

Using 6 strands of yarn 12" long for each fringe, and alternating colors, attach fringe to bottom of tote (see page 105 on fringe).

a striped scarf

Lengthwise crocheting

Size
5" x 66"

Materials
- 1 ball each of Brown Sheep
  Lamb's Pride Worsted
  85% Wool, 15% Mohair
  4 oz (113 g) – 190 yds (173 m)
  #M-03 Grey Heather (main color)
  #M-07 Sable (A)
  #M-05 Onyx (B)
- Size J-10 (6 mm) crochet hook,
  or size to get gauge

Gauge
12 stitches and 12 rows = 4" (10 cm) in half double crochet

Notes
1. When you work the beginning chain, be sure to make the loops loose. For ease in counting the number of loops in the chain, put a safety pin into the chain after 50 or 100 stitches.

2. When you add or end the yarn at the beginning or end of each row, leave a long strand, about 10", which will become part of the fringe.

Scarf
With the main color, chain 202.

Row 1 Working in the third chain from the hook, work 1 half double crochet in each chain across the row—200 half double crochets completed. Chain 2 and turn the piece.

Repeat the last row in the following stripe sequence 5 times: color A, main color, color B, main color.

Fasten off.

Fringe
Cut 20" lengths of yarn by wrapping the yarn around a firm object such as a book. Holding 2 strands of yarn together and matching the stripes in the scarf, make fringe along each short edge of the scarf. Follow fringing instructions on page 105.

a poncho

Using everything you have learned

Size
One size fits M/L

Materials
- 3 balls each of Lion Brand Wool-Ease Chunky 20% Wool, 80% Acrylic 5 oz (140 g) – 153 yds (140 m) #099 Fisherman (A) 1 ball #152 Charcoal (B) 1 ball #187 Foliage (C)
- Size K-10 1/2 (7 mm) crochet hook, or size to get gauge
- Large-eyed, blunt needle (for weaving in ends)

Gauge
3 shells and 5 rows = 4" in pattern stitch

Notes
1. This poncho is worked in a circle so that you do not have to sew a seam.

2. When working some rounds, you may want to break down the steps into smaller segments. Write down sections on index cards that you can flip over as you complete each segment. After you have made 1 or 2 rounds, it gets a lot easier.

Special stitches
Shell: (3 double crochet) in the same space.

Point Shell: (3 double crochet, chain 1, 3 double crochet) in the same space.

Abbreviations
ch = chain
dc = double crochet

Poncho
With color A, chain 84.

Join with slip stitch to first ch to form circle. This is the neck opening.

Round 1 (Neck Tie Round) Ch 3, dc in next 2 chs, ch 1, skip 1 ch, (dc in next 3 chs, ch 1, skip next ch) 4 times, (3 dc, ch 1, 3 dc) in next ch (point shell made), ch 1, skip next ch, (dc in next 3 chs, ch 1, skip next ch) 10 times, point shell in next ch, ch 1, skip next ch, (dc in next 3 chs, ch 1, skip next ch) 5

times, join with slip stitch to top of starting ch 3—10 shells between 2 point shells.

Note: For ease, mark point shells with safety pins or markers.

Round 2 Slip stitch in next 2 dc and next ch space, ch 3, 2 dc in same space, ch 1, (shell in next ch-1 space, ch 1) 4 times, point shell in ch space of point shell, ch 1, (shell in next ch-1 space, ch 1) 11 times, point shell in ch-1 space of point shell, ch 1, (shell in next ch-1 space, ch 1) 6 times, join with slip stitch to top of starting ch 3—11 shells between 2 point shells.

Round 3 Slip stitch in next 2 dc and next ch-1 space, ch 3, 2 dc in same space, ch 1, (shell in next ch-1 space, ch 1) 4 times, point shell in ch-1 space of point shell, ch 1, (shell in next ch-1 space, ch 1) 12 times, point shell in ch-1 space of point shell, ch 1, (shell in next ch-1 space, ch 1) 7 times, join with slip stitch to top of starting ch 3—12 shells between 2 point shells.

Rounds 4–17 Continue in pattern for 14 rounds more, increasing 1 shell on each side on each round. Round 17 will have 26 shells between points on each side. Fasten off A.

Rounds 18–19 Join B with slip stitch in first ch-1 space on Round 17, ch 3, 2 dc in same space. Continue in established pattern for 2 rounds (28 shells between point shells). Fasten off B.

Rounds 20–22 Join C with slip stitch in first ch-1 space on Round 19, ch 3, 2 dc in same space. Continue in established pattern for 3 rounds (31 shells between point shells). Fasten off C.

Neck Trim Turn piece around. Working in free loop of starting ch, join A with slip stitch in last ch (84th) of starting ch, ch 3, 2 dc in same space, ch 1, skip next 3 chs, (shell in next ch, ch 1, skip next 3 chs) 4 times, skip 1 more ch, shell (not point shell) in same ch as point shell on last row, ch 1, skip next 4 chs, (shell in next ch, ch 1, skip next 3 chs) 9 times, skip 1 more ch, shell (not point shell) in same ch as point shell on last row, ch 1, skip next 4 chs, (shell in next ch, ch 1, skip next 3 chs) 4 times, join with slip stitch to top of starting ch 3.

Round 2 Slip stitch in next 2 dc and next ch-1 space, ch 3, 2 dc in same space, ch 1, (shell in next ch-1 space, ch 1) around, join with slip stitch to top of starting ch 3. Fasten off A.

Neck Tie With C, ch 151, slip stitch in second ch from hook and each ch across. Fasten off C.

End Tab (Make 2) With B, ch 4, 5 dc in 4th ch from hook, ch 3, turn. Dc in each dc and top of ch 3. Fasten off B. Sew one tab to each end of tie. Thread tie through spaces on 3rd round from top (neck tie round).

Adjust to comfortable neck size and tie ends into a bow. Weave in ends.

a crocheted sweater
A chic and speedy project

Size
S (M, L)

Finished measurements
Bust 40" (44", 48")
Length 22" (23", 24")

Materials
- 10 (11, 12) skeins of Colinette/Unique Kolours Point 5, 100% Wool
  3 1/2 oz (100 g) – 55 yds (50 m)
  #55 Toscana
- Size P-15 (10 mm) knitting needles, or size to get gauge
- Large-eyed, blunt needle (for sewing)

Gauge
7 double crochet and 4 rows = 4" (10 cm)

Note
On row 2, the chain 3 (turning chain) of the previous row is the first double crochet.

Front and back
Chain 37 (41, 45).

Row 1 Double crochet in fourth chain from hook (counts as first double crochet) and in each chain across, chain 3, turn—35 (39, 43) double crochet completed.

Row 2 Double crochet in each double crochet across, chain 3, turn.

Repeat Row 2 until piece measures 13" from beginning.

Next Row Slip stitch in first 5 double crochet, chain 3, double crochet in next 26 (30, 34) double crochet, leave remaining stitches unworked, chain 3, turn—27 (31, 35) double crochet.

Next Row Double crochet in each double crochet across, chain 3, turn—27 (31, 35) double crochet.

Repeat last row until piece measures 22" (22", 23"). Fasten off.

Sleeve (Make 2)
Chain 19 (19, 21).

Row 1 Double crochet in fourth chain from hook (counts as first double crochet) and in each chain across, chain 3, turn—17 (17, 19) double crochet completed.

Row 2 (Increase Row) Double crochet in same double crochet as chain 3 (turning chain), double crochet in each double crochet across to turning chain, 2 double crochet in turning chain. Chain 3, turn—19 double crochet completed.

Row 3 Double crochet in each double crochet across. Chain 3, turn—19 double crochet.

Row 4–15 Repeat Rows 2 and 3 for 6 (6, 7) times. At the end of Row 15 you will have 31 (31, 33) double crochet. Now work even in double crochet until sleeve measures 17". Fasten off.

Finishing
Placing front and back together with the right sides facing out, sew first 4" (5", 5 1/2") across top for shoulder seam. Leave center 8" (8", 9") open for neck opening, sew last 4" (5", 5 1/2") together for other shoulder seam.

Pin top of sleeves to armhole opening, centering sleeve at the shoulder. Sew sleeves to sweater. Sew side and long sleeve seams.

Weave in ends.

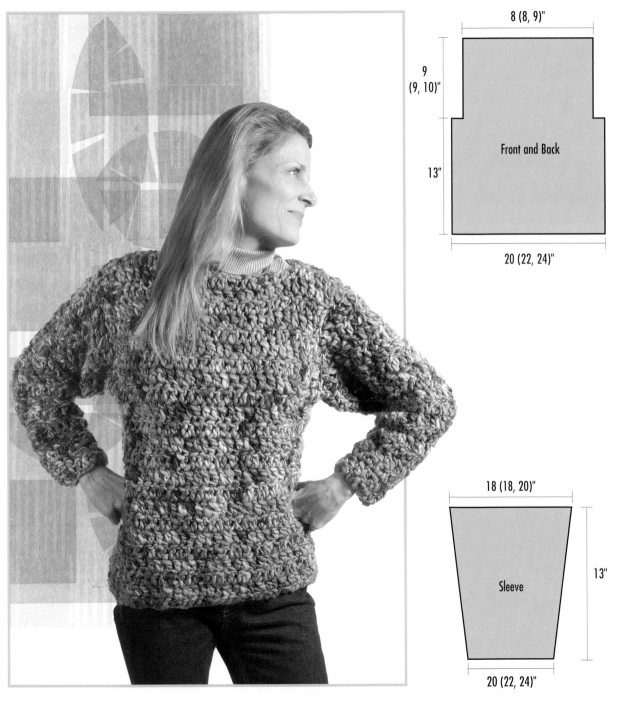

8 (8, 9)"

9
(9, 10)"

Front and Back

13"

20 (22, 24)"

18 (18, 20)"

Sleeve

13"

20 (22, 24)"

a ripple stitch baby blanket

Soft cotton in soothing baby colors

Size
36" x 30"

Materials
- 2 balls each of Lion Brand Cotton-Ease
  50% Cotton, 50% Acrylic
  3½ oz (100 g) – 207 yds (188 m)
  #169 Pistachio (A)
  #100 Vanilla (B)
  1 ball #157 Banana Cream (C)
  1 ball #156 Mint (D)
- Size H-8 (5 mm) crochet hook,
  or size to get gauge
- Large-eyed, blunt needle (for sewing squares)

Gauge
6 rows in pattern = 4" (10 cm); from one point
to the next across width = 6" (15 cm)

Color Sequence
Work [3 Rows A, 1 Row C, 3 Rows A, 4 Rows
B, 1 Row D, 4 Rows B] 3 times, end with 3
Rows A, 1 Row C, 3 Rows A—total 55 rows.

Notes
For ease in working, divide each row into sections and write individual segments on index cards. Flip the cards as you finish one section to go to the next. There are only 2 rows to remember once you have repeated rows 1–3; the remainder of the blanket is simply a repeat of rows 2 and 3.

Abbreviations
ch = chain
dc = double crochet

Blanket
With A, chain 118.

Row 1 Work dc in fifth ch from hook, ch 1, skip next ch, [dc in next ch, ch 1, skip next ch] 4 times, (dc, ch 2, dc) in next ch, *ch 1, skip next ch, [dc in next ch, ch 1, skip next ch] 4 times, yarn over, insert hook in next ch, yarn over and pull through, yarn over and pull through 2 loops on hook, skip next 2 chs, yarn over and insert hook in next ch, yarn over and pull through, yarn over and pull through 2 loops on hook, yarn over and pull through all 3 loops on hook, (decrease made), ch 1, skip next ch, [dc in next ch, ch 1, skip next ch] 4 times, (dc, ch 2, dc) in next ch, repeat from * 3 times more, ending with [ch 1, skip next ch, dc in next ch] 5 times, dc in last ch. Ch 3, turn.

Row 2 Skip first dc and ch-1 space, dc in next dc, [dc in next ch-1 space, dc in next dc] 4 times, 5 dc in ch-2 space, *[dc in next dc, dc in next ch-1 space] 4 times, [yarn over, insert hook in next dc, yarn over and pull through, yarn over and pull through 2 loops on hook] 3 times, yarn over and pull through all 4 loops on hook, (3 dc decrease made), [dc in next ch-1 space, dc in next dc] 4 times, 5 dc in ch-2 space, repeat from * 3 times more, ending with [dc in next dc, dc in next ch-1 space] 4 times, dc in next dc, skip next ch-1 space and dc, dc in top of turning chain. Ch 3, turn.

Row 3 Skip first dc, [dc in next dc, ch 1, skip next dc] 5 times, (dc, ch 2, dc) in next dc, *ch 1, skip next dc, [dc in next dc, ch 1, skip next dc] 4 times, yarn over, insert hook in next dc, yarn over and pull through, yarn over and pull through 2 loops on hook, skip next dc, yarn over and insert hook in next dc, yarn over and pull through, yarn over and pull through 2 loops on hook, yarn over and pull through all 3 loops on hook, (2 dc decrease made), ch 1, skip next dc, [dc in next dc, ch 1, skip next dc] 4 times, (dc, ch 2, dc) in next dc, repeat from * 3 times more, ending with [ch 1, skip next dc, dc in next dc] 5 times, skip next dc, dc in top of turning chain. Ch 3, turn.

Rows 4–55 Repeat Rows 2 and 3, continuing color sequence above.

At the end of Row 55, do not fasten off A. Ch 1 and turn.

Border

Single crochet in each dc and ch across Row 55. At the end of row, ch 3. Working along side of blanket, work a dc in end of Row 55, 2 dc in

end of each row to starting ch at lower edge. Working on opposite side of starting ch, single crochet in each ch across. At end of row, ch 3. Working along opposite side of blanket, dc in end of Row 1, 2 dc in end of each row to first single crochet. Slip stitch in first single crochet.

Fasten off. Weave in ends.

a quickie hat

Single crochet in the round

Gauge

5 groups of 3 double crochet = 4" (10 cm)

Notes

1. Hat is worked circularly without a seam.

2. Decreases at top of hat are made by decreasing 1 stitch as follows: single crochet 2 stitches together.

3. When working rounds to make this hat, repeat the instructions in the [ ] around the entire piece as indicated in the instructions.

Hat

With color A, chain 92 stitches and join with a slip stitch to form ring, being careful not to twist the chain.

Round 1 Chain 3, work 2 double crochet in same chain, chain 1, [skip next 3 chains, work 3 double crochet in next chain, chain 1] repeat instructions in [ ] around, joining with slip stitch to top of the beginning chain 3. Fasten off.

Round 2 Join color B with a slip stitch in the space between the first and last 3 double crochet groups, chain 3, 2 double crochet in same space, chain 1, [3 double crochet in next chain 1 space, chain 1] repeat instructions in [ ] around, joining with a slip stitch to top of the beginning chain 3. Fasten off.

Rounds 3-8 Repeat round 2 in the following color sequence: main color, A, B, main color, A, B.

Round 9 Join MC with a slip stitch in the space between first and last 3 double crochet groups, chain 3, 1 double crochet in same space, chain 1, [2 double crochet in next chain-1 space, chain 1] repeat instructions in [ ] around, joining with a slip stitch to top of the beginning chain 3. Fasten off.

Round 10 Join color A with slip stitch in space between first and last 2 double crochet groups,

Size

One size fits most adults

Materials

- 1 ball each of Lion Brand Wool-Ease 20% Wool, 80% Acrylic 3 oz (85 g) – 197 yds (180 m)
  #152 Oxford Grey (main color: MC)
  #138 Cranberry (A)
  #170 Peacock (B)
- Size G-6 (4.5 mm) crochet hook, or size to get gauge
- Large-eyed, blunt needle (for weaving in ends)

chain 4, [1 dc in next chain-1 space, chain 1] repeat instructions in [ ] around, joining with a slip stitch to third chain of the beginning chain 4. Fasten off.

Round 11 Join color B with a slip stitch in same stitch as last slip stitch, chain 1, single crochet in same stitch, single crochet in each chain-1 space around, joining with slip stitch to first single crochet. Fasten off—24 single crochet completed.

Note: From this point, work with main color to end of hat.

Round 12 Join main color with a slip stitch in first single crochet, single crochet in each single crochet around, joining with a slip stitch to first single crochet—24 single crochet completed.

Round 13 Chain 1, [single crochet 2 stitches together] repeat instructions in [ ] around, joining with a slip stitch to first single crochet—12 single crochet completed.

Round 14 Chain 1, then single crochet in each single crochet around, joining with a slip stitch to first single crochet—12 single crochet completed.

Round 15 Chain 1, [single crochet 2 stitches together around], joining with a slip stitch to first single crochet—6 single crochet completed.

Fasten off, leaving long end for sewing. Weave the end through loops of last 6 double crochet and tighten.

Fasten off.

Brim

Attach the main color with a slip stitch to foundation chain at lower edge of the hat. Work 1 single crochet in each chain around, join with a slip stitch to first single crochet, chain 1—92 single crochet completed.

Work 4 more rounds of single crochet with 92 single crochets in each round.

Fasten off. Weave in ends

F I R S T   P E R S O N   S U C C E S S   S T O R Y !

Understanding Crochet Tension

When I first started to crochet, I used the hook size recommended on the band of the yarn ball, and always ended up with stiff fabric that I didn't really like. I couldn't figure out what I was doing wrong, so I took some lessons from an expert crocheter, who explained that my natural tendency was to crochet too tightly. But instead of trying to teach me to loosen up my tension, she taught me to make soft, draping crochet fabric by using a larger hook than the one suggested. This opened the door to making sweaters, wraps, and other beautiful things, and was the key to making many successful projects regardless of the type of yarn I used. I've become really attached to my P and Q crochet hooks—they're so much easier to use and great for making quick projects.

—Katarina N., Palisades, FL

crocheted edges

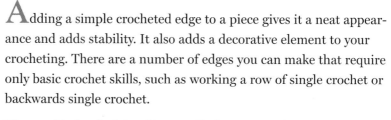

Borders that reinforce your crocheting

Adding a simple crocheted edge to a piece gives it a neat appearance and adds stability. It also adds a decorative element to your crocheting. There are a number of edges you can make that require only basic crochet skills, such as working a row of single crochet or backwards single crochet.

The two kinds of edging discussed below are stitched directly onto the crocheted fabric. You can also make separate edges and sew them onto your piece, but this requires more time and skill.

Picot edging Make one slip stitch, chain three, slip stitch into the same stitch (making a nub called a picot), work a slip stitch in next two stitches. Repeat from the beginning along or around the entire piece. It is a good idea to make one complete row or round of single crochet as a base for this edging.

Shell edging Work one single crochet, skip one or more stitches (whatever looks good and helps the piece to lie flat), work five double crochet in the chosen stitch, skip one or more stitches and repeat from the beginning along or around the entire piece.

Some edging tips:
- Work the edging evenly. This means make sure that you do not add too many stitches along the edge, which causes ruffling, or too few, which causes bunching.

- Add two or three stitches in each corner to make a neat corner turning.

- Use the same color as the project or use a contrasting yarn. When using a contrasting yarn, you might first want to work a foundation row in single crochet using the main color yarn.

- Edging can consist of one row or multiple rows, depending on the look you want to achieve.

ASK THE EXPERTS

I know that you can add edgings to blankets and home decor items, but can you use these methods on sweaters too?

Yes, and adding edges to sweaters can greatly enhance them. You can make functional edges, decorative ones, or a combination. Functional edges, such as crocheted ribbing or backward single crochet, are usually used to stabilize a sweater. For instance, you can work a row of single crochet or backwards single crochet around a neck edge to make a smooth, flat edge that is perfectly round. Decorative edges, such as shells, clusters, or scallops, can be added to the cuffs or bottom edges. And simple edges, such as several rows of single crochet, are perfect for button bands on cardigans and jackets and for stabilizing front edges. You use crochet edges not only on crocheted sweaters, but on knit sweaters as well.

No matter what I do, my edge still ripples and will not lie flat. What can I do to stop this from happening?

There are several ways to stop an edge from rippling. One way is to use a crochet hook one or two sizes smaller than the one you used to make your project. You can also skip a stitch every three or four stitches along the edge. If you skip every third stitch and it still ripples, rip out the edge and try every fourth stitch. The more you practice making edges, the easier it will be for you to make a flat edge.

I ran out of yarn when making my project, but I would like to make an edge. What can I do?

You can use another yarn to edge your project. Instead of thinking of it as a mistake, consider it a design element. Just make sure that the edging yarn has the same washing instructions as your project. It should also be approximately the same weight as the main yarn you used.

now what do I do?

Answers to common questions

I'm really nervous about choosing a project that has lots of different rows. How can I keep track of my place? Should I read the whole pattern before I begin to see if I understand what is going on?

Most patterns are less daunting if you take a step-by-step approach. You do not necessarily need to read the pattern carefully before you begin, though it's good to review unfamiliar terms and stitches, and practice them if necessary. As with a recipe, you get the best results if you go from step A to step B. It is also a good idea to complete an entire a row before you set your project aside, and to note which row you've completed. You can make a copy of the pattern and use a pen, pencil, or highlighter to make these notes. If your eyes stray from line to line, place a ruler under the line of instructions you are working on or use a magnet board with a magnet ruler to help keep your place.

I want to make a crocheted button band for a cardigan. But how do I make the buttonholes?

Making buttonholes is very easy to do when you are making a crocheted band horizontally (back and forth in rows). You simply make a chain of stitches (the number needed for the button size), leaving the stitches below the chain unworked. This makes a hole. On the next row, work the new stitches into the chain. The number of stitches you need for a buttonhole depends on the size of the button, although two to four stitches will most likely be adequate for any size button you might choose. Generally, it's best to make the buttonhole slightly small, as the fabric will stretch. If you make the buttonhole too large, you can always work slip stitch around the opening.

I bought a crochet book that includes many pattern stitches. Do I need any special skills to try out these stitches?

Most of the stitches in crochet books and magazines are just variations on the basic stitches covered in this book. Stitches worked in rows are given in multiples of stitches that are repeated across the row. For instance, a chevron stitch is worked in single crochet with multiples of 16 stitches, plus 2 extra stitches, which allows you to begin in the second chain from the hook. When working an unfamiliar stitch pattern, it's a good idea to read any stitch explanations, review the basic stitches, and practice the new stitches before you begin.

What are the best yarns to use for crocheting?

Almost any yarn used for knitting can be used to crochet. If you are new to the craft, choose yarns without texture so you'll be able to easily see the stitches and where to insert the hook to make the next stitch. This does not mean that you have to use boring yarns. You can select yarns with variations, or heathered yarns. You can also use a variety of fibers, such as wool, cotton, acrylic, or blends of these fibers. And be sure to use a yarn suitable for the project; for example, choose a soft, washable yarn for a baby project or a firm, durable yarn to make a bag. Then, once you have a few projects under your belt, you will be ready to try yarns with texture. Experiment with a few types of yarn to find out which is easiest for you to work with and which gives you the best result for your project.

NOW WHERE DO I GO?

WEB SITES

www.knitting-crochet.com

www.smartcrochet.com

www.crochetpartners.org

BOOKS

Crocheting—Kids Can Do It
By Gwen Blakely Kinsler
and Jackie Young
A book with easy, fun projects that are not just for kids!

Crochet for Tots
By Nancy Queen
Covers the basics and features 20 charming kids' designs. Also has instructions for making buttons and decorative edgings.

*Family Circle Easy Crochet:
50 Fashion and Home Projects*
By Trisha Malcolm

*Family Circle Easy Sweaters:
50 Knit and Crochet Projects*
By Trisha Malcolm
The two *Family Circle* books above are full of techniques and easy-to-make contemporary projects. Both are great additions to your crochet library.

glossary

At same time This indicates that you need to work two processes at once. For example, your pattern might say to make increases or decreases at the same time that you are following a particular stitch pattern.

Back loop In knitting, this refers to the back strand of a stitch, which your pattern may tell you to work—unlike a regular knit stitch, in which you work in the front of the loop. In crocheting, this indicates the back portion of a stitch. *See also* Front loop.

Backwards single crochet This crochet stitch, used mainly for edging, is worked in the opposite direction from a regular single crochet. It is sometimes called "reverse single crochet" or "crab stitch."

Binding off This is a technique used in knitting to end a piece. In European patterns, this is called "casting off."

Cable In knitting, this means to knit a group of stitches out of order to create a twisted, ropelike effect.

Casting on In knitting, this describes the technique used to make a foundation row of a piece.

Chain In crocheting, this is a loop made simply by drawing the yarn through an existing stitch or loop. It also refers to a series of loops; for example, your pattern might say, "chain 10," which means to make 10 chain stitches in a row.

Chain space In crocheting, this is the space created when you make a chain between two stitches.

Change to larger or smaller needles In knitting, this indicates a change in needle size. To do so, just start knitting the next row with the new needles.

Continue in pattern In both knitting and crocheting, this means to keep working the pattern following the directions for the previous rows. Also called "as established" or "in this way."

Contrasting color This is a color or several colors of yarn used as an accent. *See also* Main color.

Decrease In both knitting and crocheting, this means to subtract a stitch or stitches to shape a piece or make it narrower.

Double crochet This is a basic crochet stitch that is taller than a half-double and shorter than a triple crochet stitch.

Dye lot This refers to a large batch of yarn skeins dyed at the same time. Color varies slightly from batch to batch, so when you select yarn, use the same dye lot number to assure color uniformity in your projects.

End with a knit or right side row In a pattern, this means that once you knit the last row, you are ready to begin the next set of instructions.

End with a purl or wrong side row In a pattern, this means that once you purl the last row, you are ready to begin the next set of instructions.

Evenly spaced This means to space markers or stitches equally across a row. For example, your pattern might say, "increase 10 stitches, evenly spaced across the row."

Fasten off In crocheting, this means to end a piece. This is done by cutting the yarn and pulling it through the last loop of the piece.

Felting In this technique, fabric knitted out of animal fiber yarns is washed in hot water with agitation to create a firm, dense fabric. This process is often used to create accessories such as bags, slippers, and hats.

From beginning In both knitting and crocheting, this means "from the beginning of a piece," and is usually given with a measurement; for instance, "work in pattern until the piece measures 10" from beginning." Always measure from the very edge and place your tape measure vertically, not diagonally.

Front loop In knitting, this means to knit into the front part of the stitch (where the needle is placed to make a regular knit stitch). In crocheting, this indicates the front part of a stitch. *See also* Back loop.

Foundation chain In crochet, this is the first row of chains upon which the piece is worked.

Garter stitch In knitting, this is a stitch in which every row is knit. When working garter stitch with a circular needle, you must knit 1 row and purl 1 row.

Gauge In both knitting and crocheting, gauge is a measurement that helps you achieve the correct size for your piece. Most often, gauge is indicated in a pattern as the number of stitches and rows over a specific measurement (usually 4" square) which you should try to make. Sometimes gauge is called "tension," especially in British patterns.

Gauge swatch A 4" (10 cm) square sample that you knit or crochet before starting a project to ensure that the piece will be correctly sized.

Group This refers to a series of stitches that are considered a unit. This term is used in crocheting when making stitches such as shells or clusters.

Half double crochet A crochet stitch that is taller than single crochet and shorter than double crochet.

Increase In both knitting and crocheting, this means to add a stitch or stitches in order to shape or widen a piece.

Knitwise This describes a way of slipping a stitch from one needle to the other. This is done by inserting the needle into the stitch as if you were going to knit it. *See also* Purlwise.

Loop In both knitting and crocheting, this is one stitch. For instance, crochet instructions might say, "yarn over and draw through a loop," meaning a stitch.

Main color The dominant color of yarn used for a project. *See also* Contrasting color.

Make 1 In knitting, this is an increase made by making a new stitch between two stitches. Because it is invisible, make 1 is a very common increase.

Motif In crocheting, a motif (or "medallion") is a circular or square piece joined with other pieces to create a whole project. For instance, a granny square is a motif. It is also used in knitting to describe a pattern (usually a colorwork one), such as a Norwegian snowflake motif.

Multiple(s) This indicates that a number of stitches in one pattern repeat. For example, your pattern might say, "a multiple of 6 knit stitches, plus 1 extra, 4 times." This means that you would repeat these directions four times, for a total of 24 stitches plus 1 stitch.

Next row In a pattern, this indicates that after you complete the current row, the next row will have different directions. Often the pattern will say, "next row (RS)" or "next row (WS)." This tells you whether you will be working a right side (RS) or wrong side (WS) row.

Pick up and knit This term is used in reference to adding edges onto a finished piece. Instead of picking up a loop from the finished fabric, you wrap the yarn around the needle and draw a loop up through the edge.

Place a marker In knitting, this means to put a ring marker onto the needle in order to set off a group of stitches. In crocheting and sometimes in knitting, placing a marker can also be done by putting an open ring marker or safety pin into the fabric. Markers can also be used to identify the front and back sides of a piece, or a specific area, such as the beginning of an arm-hole.

Ply (plies) This refers to the number of individual fiber strands that make up a strand of yarn, such as "four-ply." Note that a larger number of plies does not necessarily mean a thicker yarn, because the fiber strands used may be extremely thin.

Purlwise This describes a way of slipping a stitch from one needle to the other. The stitch is slipped by inserting the needle into the stitch as if to purl it. *See also* Knitwise.

Rep from * to end In both knitting and crocheting, this means to repeat the instructions that follow the symbol * to the end of the row or round. *See also* Rep between **.

Rep between ** In both knitting and crocheting, this sets off an instruction chain to be repeated up to a certain point in the pattern. Double asterisks are often used when single asterisks are already in use.

Reverse shaping In both knitting and crocheting, this indicates that a second piece is made as a mirror image of the first piece for symmetry. Reverse shaping is most often used to create separate left and right front sides for cardigans and jackets.

Reverse stockinette stitch In knitting, this is a stitch made by purling the right-side rows and knitting the wrong-side rows. It is sometimes called "reverse jersey." *See also* Stockinette stitch.

Ribbing This knitting stitch pattern, made of a combination of knit and purl stitches, results in an elastic edge. Common ribbing stitch patterns include knit 1, purl 1, and knit 2, purl 2. Sometimes ribbing is used in crocheting to mimic knit ribbing patterns.

Right side The front side of a piece. "Right side row" is a common term used in both knitting and crocheting. *See also* Wrong side.

Round In both knitting and crocheting, this is a row that is made in a circle.

Row This refers to a series of consecutive stitches; the length of a row is the length of one side of your piece. *See also* Stitch.

Selvage (selvedge) These are edge stitches that are used to keep a piece from rolling, or to make a neat line for seaming.

Single crochet A basic crochet stitch that is taller than a slip stitch and shorter than a half double crochet.

Slip stitch The shortest basic crochet stitch, this "nonstitch" is made by pulling a loop through an existing stitch. Because it adds little height to a piece, it is often used to join rounds. It is also used to make firm edgings.

Ssk (slip, slip, knit) A decrease that slants to the left, the ssk is made by slipping two stitches from the left needle to the right as if you were knitting them (knitwise), and then knitting them together through the front loops of the stitches. One stitch is decreased using this method.

Ssp (slip, slip, purl) A decrease that slants to the left, the ssp is made by slipping two stitches from the left needle to the right needle as if you were knitting them (knitwise). You then slip them back to the left needle and purl them together through the back loops of the stitches. One stitch is decreased using this method.

Stitch In both knitting and crocheting, this refers to one individual unit worked horizontally and interlocked with the next one. In knitting, stitches are held on a needle and worked in rows. In crocheting, stitches are worked individually, and only one is held on the hook at all times. *See also* Row.

Stockinette stitch In knitting, this stitch, also known as "jersey," is made by knitting on right-side rows and purling on wrong-side rows.

Stranding In this multicolor knitting technique, sometimes called "Fair Isle," one or several strands of yarn are carried along the back of a piece until it is used again.

Swatch This is a small knitted or crocheted sample made to determine the correct gauge for the project. *See also* Gauge.

Tail This is a length of yarn left over after you cast on (knitting) or make a foundation chain (crocheting). The tail is later woven into the finished fabric or may be used to make a seam.

Tension In both knitting and crocheting, this describes how tightly or loosely you make your stitches. The tension you tend to use correlates directly with the size of the finished piece. *See also* Gauge.

Triple (treble) crochet This is the tallest of all the basic crochet stitches.

Turning chain In crocheting, this refers to the number of chains you must make before beginning the next row to ensure that a row is the correct height. Turning chain instructions are given either at the end of a row or at the beginning of the next row.

Weaving in ends In both knitting and crocheting, this means to work in a yarn tail by weaving it in and out of the finished fabric. In patterns, this is often the last instruction indicated.

Work as for back In both knitting and crocheting, this is most often used to explain how to work the front piece of a sweater. It indicates that you should follow the exact same instructions as you used to make the back piece. For example, your pattern may read, "work as for back until armhole measures 8".

Work even In both knitting and crocheting, this means to continue in a pattern without any further increases or decreases. For example: "work even until piece measures 5".

Work to end In both knitting and crocheting patterns, this means to continue with your pattern stitch to the end of the row or round.

Wrong side The back of a piece. *See also* Right side.

Yarn over In knitting, this is an increase that makes a hole, which is done by wrapping the yarn over the needle. This technique is often used in lace patterns. In crocheting, "yarn over" means to wrap the yarn around the hook and pull up a loop.

ABBREVIATIONS/SYMBOLS

( ) = Work the instructions within the parentheses as many times as directed. Also used to set off sizing within a pattern, for example: Small (Medium, Large, X-Large).

[ ] = Work the instructions within the square brackets as many times as directed.

* = Repeat the instructions following the single asterisk as directed. For example, *k1, p1; repeat from * to end.

** = Repeat the instructions between asterisks as many times as directed or repeat from a given set of instructions. For example, *k1, p1, **k2, p2; repeat from * once, then repeat from ** to end.

Abbreviations

approx = approximately

beg = begin(ning)

CC = contrasting color

ch = chain

ch-sp = chain space
(often written as ch-1 sp)

cn = cable needle

CO = cast on

cont = continue

dc = double crochet

dc2tog = double crochet 2 stitches together (decrease)

dec = decrease(s)(ing)

foll = follow(s)(ing)

hdc = half double crochet

inc = increase(s)(ing)

k = knit

k2tog = knit 2 together

kwise = knitwise

LH = left hand
(as in left-hand needle)

lp(s) = loop(s)

M1 = make one (increase)

MC = main color

p = purl

pat(s) = pattern(s)

pm = place marker

psso = pass slip stitch over knit stitch (decrease)

p2tog = purl 2 together

pwise = purlwise

rem = remain(s)(ing)

rep = repeat

rev St st = reverse stockinette stitch

RH = right hand
(as in right hand needle)

rib = ribbing

rnd = round

RS = right side

sc = single crochet

sc2tog = single crochet 2 stitches together (decrease)

sk = skip

SKP = slip 1, knit 1, pass slip stitch over knit stitch (decrease)

sl = slip

sl marker = slip marker

sl st = slip stitch

sp = space

ssk = slip 1, slip 1, knit these 2 stitches together (decrease)

st(s) = stitch(es)

St st = stockinette stitch

t-ch = turning chain

tbl = through back loop

tog = together

tr = triple or treble crochet

WS = wrong side

wyib = with yarn in back

wyif = with yarn in front

yo = yarn over

yo2 = yarn over twice

Weights and Measures Abbreviations

cm = centimeter(s)

g or gm = gram(s)

m = meter(s)

mm = millimeter(s)

oz = ounce(s)

yd(s) = yard(s)

in, " = inch(es)

Note

Yarn for the projects in this book was provided by:

Brown Sheep Co.
100662 Country Road 16
Mitchell, NE 69357

Crystal Palace Yarn
160 23rd St.
Richmond, CA 94804
510-237-9988
www.straw.com

Lion Brand Yarn Company
34 West 15th St.
New York, NY 10011
800-258-9276
www.lionbrand.com

Reynolds
35 Scales Lane
Townsend, MA 01469-1094
978-597-8794

Tahki/Stacy Charles Inc.
8000 Cooper Ave., Bldg. 1
Glendale, NY 11385
800-338-9276
www.tahkistacycharles.com

Unique Kolours
Colinette Yarns
28 North Bacton Hill Rd.
Malvern, PA 19355
800-252-3934
www.uniquekolours.com

index

ABOUT THE AUTHOR

Nancy J. Thomas developed a lifelong interest in needlework when she was mentored in the needle arts by her Canadian grandmother. This fascination later turned into a career. She was formerly the editor of *Knitter's Magazine* and style director for a number of knitting-related books published by *Knitter's Magazine*. She is the former editor of *Vogue Knitting*, was the founding editor of *Family Circle Knitting*, and was instrumental in the launch of *Vogue Knitting Magazine* in 1982. Nancy is currently the editorial director for Lion Brand Yarn Company, and is the coauthor of *Vogue Knitting: The Ultimate Knitting Book* and *A Passion for Knitting*. In her free time she knits!

BARNES & NOBLE BASICS™

Barbara J. Morgan Publisher

Barb Chintz Editorial Director

Leonard Vigliarolo Design Director

Wynn Madrigal Senior Editor

Leslie Stem Design Assistant

Emily Seese Editorial Assistant

Monique Boniol Photo Researcher

Della R. Mancuso Production Manager

Barnes & Noble Books would like to thank the following consultants for their help in preparing this book: **Barbara Breiter**, coauthor of *The Complete Idiot's Guide to Knitting & Crocheting Illustrated* (*Second Edition*). Her patterns are available at **www.knitabit.net** and she also runs an extensive knitting Web site at **http://knitting.about.com**; **Elisa Williams**, a journalist in San Francisco, CA, who began knitting at age five and enjoys tackling complicated lace and cable patterns; **Judy Williams**, who teaches knitting to elementary and high school students in Redding, CA, and has traveled abroad extensively to study traditional knitting designs; and **Marianne Forestal**, who designed and made a number of the crocheted projects featured in this book.

ART CREDITS

Glee Barre All step-by-step illustrations

Robert Milazzo All model photography

Ellen Barasch Photo stylist for model photography

Artfibers: 4 (bottom), 6, 20, 26, 27, 38, 74, 90, 130; **Clover Needlecraft, Inc.:** 30, 32; **Coats & Clark**: 40; **Corbis**: 24 bottom **Don Mason**, 25 bottom **Richard Hamilton Smith**; **Crystal Palace Yarns**: 21; **Jack Deutsch**: 7, 39, 55, 75, 91, 109, 131, 175; **Kaleidoscope Yarns**: 16; **Gwen Blakley Kinsler**: 43; **Lion Brand®Yarn Company**: 1, 2, 3, 51, 22, 33, 35, 113; **Private Collection of Agnes Oslander**, Canada, BC/Photography by **Ernst Oslander**: 11; **Rowan Yarns**: 5 (top and middle), 14; **Judy Williams**: 12; **The Woolie Ewe**: cover, 155